Broken Sleep Books is a working-class indie publisher putting access to the arts at the forefront of what we do. We continue to endeavour to dismantle gentrification within creative arts industries, and one of the core principles of Broken Sleep is in our desire to ensure we are involved in community action: Whether fundraising, mentoring, our giving away books to those in need.

Selected Anthologies from Broken Sleep Books

2024 Anthology

Edited by:
Aaron Kent & Stuart McPherson

ISBN: 978-1-916938-68-7

Cover designed by Aaron Kent

Edited by Aaron Kent & Stuart McPherson

Typeset by Aaron Kent

Broken Sleep Books Ltd
Rhydwen
Talgarreg
Ceredigion
SA44 4HB

Broken Sleep Books Ltd
Fair View
St Georges Road
Cornwall
PL26 7YH

CONTENTS

POETRY

January

HOMUNCULUS WITH MILK TOOTH

All of the teeth that will ever be in my head
are in my head   lined up like slow cows
in pink flesh   improbable carillon

in my skull's belfry   where they wobble
and chime   dull   dull   each
little hammer   against my tongue

my gums are emptying   spat teeth
under my pillow   mouth full of
nothing   clammy wattles   spent

NIGHT FEED WITH SUMMER SOLSTICE

Are they different, the winter's children?
Held tighter in the diurnal maw? Light
stirred less thick in the blood?

Two hours across the squandering dawn
I've tricked this ounce of milk to the small cave
in the pebble of your gut, and what luck
the day we're growing into

— the peach of it, the dove coo'd size of the thing
rearing up improbable as a giraffe's head
all eyes and wide cheeked in her stall.
Morning

and somewhere else night falls
on the other side of the year. Our days
lessen while theirs unfrond.
Things tip inevitably back to the centre

this room, the hour. Awake
my long breath in your ear calms you.
Yours is hot and short in mine.

DESIRE | LEISURE CENTRE

O | men of the swimming pool changing room | give me
your panting | wet breath charged with your lungs' blood
| that has kissed your heart through a gauze | thin
as a wedding veil | you fresh from the pool | marshalling
your clouds of spent air | let me gather them | such exhalations
your vocal chords sing | the *uh* of labour | the *uh*
of investment | and you in the shower | slick and whistling
your hot and coursing life | whistle to me | I will stitch it
with these others | men of the swimming pool changing room
permit me | I shall wear your panting | a garment
of sighs | beneath this hasty workshirt | warm | it shall cover me
tonight | by morning they shall mist my window | these tiny beads
you have laced me with | and I thank you | I thank you

I'll share a secret
Ash white, auspiciously wild
In the kitchen
In the bed
In the spa
Fucking
Big
Small
Young
Old
Just as I come
To remind myself
To direct the energy
This is what
I finally
Say

Thousand and

Now I know that you and I

Meet intimately

In this sound

Always

Here

       Dog

            God

Scratched behind the ear

Sometimes after
The lightning smile

Sometimes after
Coming cloudy white on a pink hole, then pushing it inside

Sometimes after
Hehe

Sometimes after
Fuck yeah

Sometimes after
The fresh smell of pine

Sometimes after
The musky smell in pubic hair

Sometimes after
The taste of tangy-salty sperm

Sometimes after
The touch of the cool breeze

Open, clear

(I) TEMPO

Like gods,

As gods,

Gods,

We were,

Happy, for a time,

Runs fast,

Runs still,

Runs out.

The price of pomegranate split,

Then savoured,

A harvest, twice stolen,

Can never be returned.

Spoil and soldier of unwinnable war,

The undodgeable draft,

Willing or unwilling,

We shall be led to drink.

AN INEXHAUSTIVE LIST OF LOVERS
(to be appended ad infinitum)

A comically repressed, archetypally English boy at a house party the other night, who I'm half convinced is an actual spy. An absolute sweetheart of a porn star, who told me about his plans to become a consultant, then kissed me on the hand when I said goodnight. An actor I had seen in a Fringe play weeks earlier—googled him the night before a party and found myself introduced to him while dancing. A nice girl with a bleach blonde buzz cut, who, while I was on my break during a particularly hard bartending shift, offered to make me dinner 'sometime' (Thank you. I love you. Come find me). An eccentric baby-faced actor at an out-of-town party, with whom I was deliriously forward—I kissed him and he let me sleep on his shoulder on the coach home. A tall, stunning girl in a club basement—with an outfit for years—whose friend I kissed to pacify him, and to keep her in the vicinity. Boy with the kind of face that drives all the boys crazy. Danced all night and now I can't stop thinking about that fucking face my god...! Charming, musical theatre piano-playing virtuoso in a Greenwich village dive bar, took my $5 tip with his teeth. Another actor, with hidden depths—The kind of boy that's desirous of everything and everyone, and desired by everything and everyone. Girl with long blue hair, a shade I can't quite describe, and a fur trim on an impeccable winter coat that matched said hair perfectly. A man who is, quite simply, far better than he knows. [REDACTED]. One boy winks, and angels orgy to harpsichord in minor. Him, skin pale and sickly as greeting card paper, yet eyes and face shining as an emperor. A man on the Hammersmith and City line with tattoos peeking through the sleeves of his suede jacket, and a face like one of the great war poets — quiet and sad and resolute and gay — one I imagine in his verses euphemistically calls the fever he feels for other men "an ague." A tree surgeon—last spotted suspended above Bethnal Green Road—with the rosiest cheeks I have ever seen. Young man whose barely whispered compliment about my earring I would have missed, had I not been so desperately waiting for him to say absolutely anything—

FRAGMENT #14

Is there not world enough for us,

Or is there too much world?

The heart beats,

Wants to beat,

But the rib cage,

Constrains the heart,

The flesh constrains the ribcage,

The constitution falters,

Air cannot hope to rout such blight,

Foul dust pumps into extremities,

Pray now only for miracles of amber.

Even the most unliving fossil,

Once strode the world,

In search of touch and succour,

Entreated some connection.

There is an appeasement,

A balm,

Something that is called to fill it,

For every aching gap.

Believe you me.

Life calls itself into existence,

Out of a mirror universe of nothings.

We wrote the bible, the God, and the man.

Built the garden,

Then banished ourselves from it.

What might we still do now,

That midnight calls at our door?

[HOW SHE GOT MADE]

I remember being afraid of AN ENSEMBLE TO DIE FOR so I would pull my covers up AGAINST ERGONOMICS.

I remember cracking THE MAYHEM FACTORY on the floor at swimming and not knowing THE LORDS OF DISCIPLINE.

I remember WRITING A SLASHER-MOVIE SEQUEL in a cupboard with my brother for hours until our mum thought we were lost.

I remember making A DICKENS OF A TASK with my brothers and daring THE ANATOMY OF A FROG.

I UNLEASHED THE GOBLINS in the night but AFTER SAYING GOODBYE we got caught. (Every time).

I remember when THE HEART let me hold YOUR OWN INCOMPETENCE!

[SAMPLE DIALOGUES]

A different way of asking
                    CLOSED/OPEN
It sounds like you're stuck - powerful questions tend to
stop people.
                    WHY DON'T YOU CARE?

A narrow tunnel that usually leads to inside / out.
A rope is called an anchor,
            to the edge of improbability.

                              NOTE: there are times when *alive* will be
                                  very dramatic and times when it will be
                                                       very quiet.

You see a historical pattern of trouble. Where do you
abandon yourself?
At the same time, it's worth celebrating when this happens.
//////////////////////////////Disconnecting?   *Say so.*

[TIME TRAVEL]

From the fierce &
wonderful, ARE WE MOST PRODUCTIVE?

(Follow me here)

Some sort of narrative? I can feel -
THE COLD EARTH - far from those I loved.

He asks 200 years ago - 'how long will this posthumous existence of mine last?'

I hold it towards him. IT'S TIME
I GOT ON WITH IT.

A fresh spinning of a story -
       what a set of people
              we live amongst.

TOUGH GUY

It snowed that year. I know because I've studied
the camcorder footage that was unearthed,
trying to pick you out of the muddied
jostle but finding you uncaptured,
just out of shot. I imagine how the mud
dug into your soles as you stampeded
the field, piled into the row in front and vaulted
the rusted bars of the iron gate. How it thawed
at the edges of the ditch you dunked
in, steeped waist-high in its colour and cold.
How it bloodied, not far from the barbed
wire crawl where a few got their head
and shoulders nicked flinching from a live round.
How it smeared thick the tunnels most travelled,
the surest exits. How it pulped into matted
heaps of burnt hay and dung, clogged
the braids of ropes you clung to, filled
your nostrils, ears and fingernails, blathered
your numbered white T-shirt, and printed
a hand on the cup of tea that steamed
the lens and scorched your lip at the race's end.

AMATEUR GARDENER

It's foolish of me
but I'm keeping you alive as the bay tree.

I have you standing guard
in the sheltered front garden,

confined to a cracked pot
too small to root,

but leafing larger every year;
shading what goes on in here.

When your leaves yellow, I pick them off,
let fall to the breathing moss

that has grassed-in the trunk:
a haphazard clump of mulch.

Afraid you'll prosper
or die back altogether,

I stop myself from digging deep
and potting up.

Best not to break the pot
and prise you out:

soils, cells, vitals,
root ball and all.

And talking to you,
like all sensible gardeners do,

seems out of the question;
a fool's experiment in suppression.

No, better to prune and pine
and bide my time

watering till you bubble and overflow.
Ridiculous, I know.

SELF-PORTRAIT WITH BARI

in rhythm   *i dream he*   is breath-hot   *is fire*

    in hunger   *i leap out*   in neon   is knowing   *the window*

is owl-eyed   *i chase him*   in sweat-glow   *through alleys*

    is shattered   *a smoke trail*   in chordage   *i can't see*   in evening

i call out   in rhythm   *from doorways*   is stagelight   *i listen*   in violence

    he crackles   is owl-eyed   is breath-hot   *i conjure*   in grasping

my bari   is orphaned   *i bellow*   in neon   *he blazes*   in violence

    then quiet   is grasping   *then darkness*   is orphaned   *i touch him*

in chordage   *my lips burn*   in sweat-glow   *become him*

    in stagelight   is shattered   *on all fours*   is hunger

is knowing   *my body*   in evening   *is fire*

EVENING SKETCH: AFTER EAVAN BOLAND

echoes where chambers   where voices

join palms   my daughter where kneeling blue

eye-paint where alms   candescence where aching

where snowmelt   is warm   Dublin's night-cold

where burning & absence   where song / un-

photoed where pitch-black   our torchlights where

aching   where drums pound   the whispers our

torchlights where dancing where   arms are deception

a god strikes wher- / ever   cups where more cups: the night holds

my daughter   huddled   where drums pound   our echoes

where burning   *i see you*: an island   my daughter

the kneeling   snowmelt's candescence where

absence is alms / de-   ception where feathers, cicadas,

late Brahms   where huddled un-photoed   a lone bulb where

warm   now absence   affliction & pitch-black

join palms   cups where more cups: a god strikes

alone   Dublin's voices where chambers   blue

torchlights here-   after / our   whispers

my daughter re-   feather your song

IN BED

he cannot
  not pretend
the late-night

winter wind
  is her slum-
brous breathing

beside him
  in the empty
dark again

February

THE EMERGENCES, THE PAUSE

The difficulty of narrating anything to you at all

This is we leaving the cinema

Feeling at the tipping point to fact

Mini-worlds will, as we are wont to hear, spin to a minimal music

Much of our afternoons filled with laughter and socialism

The emergences, the pause

Between this sentence and the next takes years

In between, a cryo-frozen brain is linked back to a body

Which at first feels the need to yawn

Cut to another yawn

Then another

Until dailiness is a mouth

The musical equivalent of

THEN WE DREAM YOU TOGETHER

Arc to narrative arc subtends

You have the awe of someone who cannot remember

If the atmosphere imperceptible to actors
where a comma hangs
were we to pause in air

Where to change our way of speaking
is to change our lives

To wake and find our speeches in the air

Trope by frayed trope
an account of morning

You have the awe of someone who cannot forget

Trembling before the marvels of industry

Then we dream you together
trembling with excitement

You have the awe of someone

Else, devoured by ornament
we change our lives

To wake and find us sutured to a place
and by waking tug the atmosphere
with our skin

Arch to arch subtends

You have the awe of someone else

Scissioned from your skin

To wake and understand you need this in your life
so speak it lovingly

You have someone else's awe
so speak it, lovingly

Trope by trope
our frayed speech

Before the marvels of industry

To wake and understand you need this in your life
so want for it a prosody

1. nevertheless it's clear
how quiet the woods are here
seen from the front
2. among the trees I come to four
always the same not
comparable
among the trees I come to four
always the same not
comparable
surely therefore from right
to left a coat
which you want to show
so go on show
3. starting point
4. they'll probably leave today
he's wearing the same

as when they came
1. the actress is right
they'll probably leave today
he's wearing the same
as when they came
2. on the one hand
I think you should go
on the other hand
you can't stay still either
when no one hears you
the grass
behind the green table
mousey men who fall in love
with young girls
unaware of their existence
3. nevertheless it's clear

how quiet the woods are here
seen from the front
4. through the middle of the field
a road
until someone had the idea
to look on the other side
after all there's woods there too
1. at the circumference of the tree
the father and mother lie near the tent
an extenuating circumstance
they fell asleep
2. rehearsal
always in the distance that lorry
the brass band isn't in uniform
there's no way they can meet
they're all going at the same speed

An aerial view of tributaries that
maps the source for the deep
end the dive into swimming pool
wearing weights around ankles
mimics the feeling of drowning. If
you press on my stomach, touch
on each individual tributary to see
which date was missed.

I can't sleep for thinking about
falling – no, maybe diving, the clots
in my menstrual cup dropping at a
different rate than the descending
chromatic scale of my blood.
Unmentioned - menses - red exact
date. Today I bleed onto my skirt,
nobody can tell. I wish I had worn
white.

absence when do you not call / that wait / the paper remains white / cramps feel rumour heavy / you deliberately looking at me ~~you are not there~~ / caress the bed / roll onto the vulva warm space / feel the shape of your swell ~~you are not there~~ / bear down / fuck me from behind / squat over bath / work schedule interrupted by internal calendar / my feelings transparent as marble skin ~~you are not there~~ / the feeling of narrow when you are unwell / swimming pool / deep end

FLUBBERGUST

can't come out today—
bit of a mad one

i was opening a packet of crisps
and found a blue whale inside

i said: normally the packaging
is inside *you*

but he failed to see the funny side

i called a number
on the crisp packet
but i don't think the girl was listening

she said it should go out with the general waste

i said for the love of god

it's still alive

THE APPRENTICESHIP

i arrived there at ten to eight in the morning,
an industrial estate just off junction 4.
i parked my bike, straightened my shirt,
and knocked – three times as instructed.

a man opened the door, introduced himself as Matthew.
he'd spent his whole life manufacturing doors,
said it was the best job in the world
as no two doors are the same,

in that no two doors will open into or out of
the same space, to the same people, at the same time.

over the next three months Matthew taught me
everything he knew (about doors, at least).
until one day, he didn't show up.
the next day he didn't show up either.

i went to his house. knocked
and called his name and waited.
no answer so i let myself in.

inside, all the doors—on cupboards,
on cabinets, on wardrobes—were open;
Matthew had been looking for something.

they found his car a few days later
—all the doors were open—but they never found him.

ANY DAY NOW

when the sun rises you best be ready.
a passport, a gun, five thousand dollars.
keep telling yourself you can start anew.
life begins in your head. count to ten.

a passport, a gun, four thousand dollars.
you must follow the system. please sign here.
keep telling yourself nothing is real.
it will never happen to you.

you're not on the system. please wait here.
a finger presses a panic button.
what happens next is anybody's guess.
the sound of rain. the aftermath.

a finger squeezes, a trigger, deletes.
air escapes your lungs, birds fly.
the sound of rain. and after that?
the sun rises, a new day starts.

THE RETURN
 for Jordan

I brought it back. What weren't we waiting for? You winked like a kind of clear moon, tarot too hard to read. Invoked stricture, charts of the flaming, the womb. And I don't have a sensibility to share – I care less about stars than smiles, the close-up of Lover's face, you know? We share that, the beach a cheaper ring, toy-ruby and rusted nail, two-strung curl the tunnel of the train like woods a hollow warping leaves so light, symmetry or parallax from the pines many lines so threads of silver, rust, the ring morning-stretched as Lover intended! I follow mops of green – I follow the way you face day in moon, Pictland, the world a wood. Miss your tongue. Escape to where the scene cannot reach, slope and track and reverse slope, leaves envisioned in grass' hair ruffled by the winds like some faint hand, a stray tap and carry and flow on ponds painted by flowers gestu-reflecting come summer, purple or amber or teal. To see a spot and think, I love you. Tomato seeds. Give me totem, give me pleasure, give me permission, just because, ecstatic trots calmed by the walk-weary weight of Inverness, her firm press to suitcase, the warm face of Three Graces –

Faith! Chance! Memory!

Inverness to Linlithgow, July 2020 (12th)

BEAUTIFUL MOTH CAPTURED IN GLASS THEN RELEASED!!!!!!!!!!!!

I

a)

Used [i]non-
places[/i] 2
capture the flow
of ur response
battering smol air
wi a long see
-thru knot

b)

Took pictures
wowed via glass
in ur stretch of space
(capsule-object) coz
ur ammonitic front
turned wi cup 2 face
the metal eye in my blind hand

c)

Window opened 2 far
as if a door
2 sell the light from
in the morning

this night &
u flew to the concrete
side of the sill

II

Albino barked wi lichen fans

WHILE EATING PRINGLES (OR, WORLD MESSAGE)

– whisper, regardless, to (

> *poppy in chorus of green wheat*
> *rain-speckled whisker | threading*
> *-coloured chandelier | playpark*
> *tree hair monocombed along honey*
> *-light | shadow taller than rainbow*
> *trunk anchor-horizon | clouded*
> *assurance paint-peach soap*
> *bubble adrift whirl-motion*
> *-cream-paint-tendril-whatever O*
> *blush grey edge vacuum-flush*
> *|| streetlight dawn super-low orb*
> *|| earliest train under*
> *silver gates // Go*

) type my message on coal
one swipe from the worst
websites. Clouds conjugate

spaceships above, salt diamonds
clicked to place only my soft
pink parabola, ever-tasting,

                                        in silence –

Springfield, Linlithgow, August 2014 (24th)

March

PENCIL

At the back of the building sacks empty
lemon fills my eyes with tears; such is
the music of restoration in your hands
spread like teeth before a blind composer.
Faultless drizzle from the fountain cuts
arches about you: anxiety hangs in it
ripe for my bunches of fingers; alert
it pulls the white stick, the fox is afraid,
low cloud obscures your last envelope. Carry
what you can, outline your eyes with poppyseed
as you leave me. I'll wait in the kitchen.
Sweet houseflies will predict the dissolution
of an order from this heap of patois: only
outside a pencil stalks the implacable day.

CROSSING
for Lara Pawson

On a street on a wall with him and without him
or are we part of that word wandering? His feet
knowing had been through one place to another
for no one knew in that going only just the street
to look away fallen to the city, our need close by.

Keys of language, the liberties I heard would help
her because a world will never remit the one door
that level open rest over so far and so many weeks
of raw majority no bare earth or grub for food or
water by word or gesture not what she has left.

Destined to become is a negative worn down by
blood as we say as we were due to come home
we could no longer no longer remain on the earth
when we left them for dead in limpid water and
all it is said to offer and disintegrate and nail us.

It was not kind, a poisonous leak of hope as a
direct hit on need and fault and what can't help
who or what in knots of wire like faces and faces
like wire full of distance complete and near grief
to explode over again no chance to bind the cut.

To trim up for refuge brimmed grief so to hand
and always to fall back to harm of the living, as
we were born and are deep in us in the world as
a flight from what it is to what it is and find no
respite set in motion but fear of dying out of it.

POEM FOR NUMBERS

They fold into themselves turn
to such days seen in what follows
as my feelings to your ten cares
quite badly and funny and dry

      show him how
      angel of words
      about not being
      so many things

madly writing to the long sob
of fatal haunts and boiled chicken
to flap the biggest shape
in an identity parade

how far I am without so much
as French closing as it touched
a mark to count on the tongue
left to ourselves at vespers

as they said this copy is
for me, a masterpiece of mind
whispers in my ear in the manner
of a split minute to you

if they add up, a word of morning
a far place on my fingers
you know I'll be about to pour
the floods of our life

      on to the word sky
      an impulse to talk
      voices into figures
      to measure ourselves

hans memling

descent includes extra   the reminder

heresies express   the invisible

devotion to   feasting destruction of

an establishment lucky to live in such a terrible age

the destitute dying in get-rich-quick cities

       the meeting at the golden gate

       the unlucky bridge   the garden

passageway to

alleluia

the council of ephesus   look out

look out

the swirling & jaunty promises of graduation degrade

       a mourning diary

       an enclosed order

[the angel kneels]

a bench a little terrace a

rug   lush with fidget toys   the invisible

lake drained long ago   who goes

here without reason goes

chronic & characteristic of

        mirrors wrapping careers as though

these are reasons   the rational

thumb sucking of winning

        that tunnel wind forces

        back the origins

the wrong of claiming nothing for the losing

way of knowing

                what is wrong & waking it

patronage is wooded landscape   a holy &

giotto

directives of drama construct the choir
          to begin the curtains
chants whether the dawning
compartmentalisation   the existing
acting out above what acts out below
          a stationary working out
vested in oratory sanctification
                    the dust bowl of
specificity   the necessarily linked charms
private & surrounded   roll up
the shown are each
          right angles to the body
that niche of decorative song
                    between

I. NOCTURNE/ AUBADE

Where to begin but night

as high tide, lush with kelp,

licks at the harbour wall

and a lone oystercatcher

ghosts its underside out

beyond the pier's crook.

A scrum of small boats

hunker on the breath

of the swell's accordion

and chimes of halliard

on staysail toll this midnight.

From the pier-end saltire,

turn to see the small town

fold itself into the brae

beyond the quayside,

snake in soda-light up

towards the Free Church,

on past the Dreel Hall

and shop, to the warmth

of upper-town bungalows,

where native Gamrie sleeps

in its Doric entitlement.

Let your gaze wander back

to a sea pinned with starlight

and washed in moon-silver,

stained with alluvium

from the day's storm.

Deep in the shore's bones,

the tide's abiding question

remains unanswered, as waves

milk the cliffs of their foam,

and the bay's gargled vowel

is rinsed in their wake.

Listen closely and you will hear

the hollow pock of pebbles

under the draw of backwash,

as the swell smooths out its folds

on Gardenstown beach

and time pauses upon

the lone comma of a seal snout

punctuating the night's rucked

canvas. Back to Seatown,

where the light's asklint

in *Harbour Cottage*, Zander's

silhouette bidding farewell

to his wine-wasted Juliet.

Watch him stagger, the reel

of this versioned drunk:

a poor wandering *mannie*

adrift on his intemperance.

Tomorrow, he will wake

to the tide's reaffirmation,

to the hiss between its teeth

and the day's new music

brogued into being

by these dialects of water.

The moon overprints itself
upon the block of this night,
sheens sillion onto roof slate
and ghosts among the lanes
of the sleeping town.
For now, it's time to go
dispel the klatch of redshank
jittering on the wharf,
to stroll its landward length
and take this seeing home
to a sleeping child and mother
wrapped in one another,
aground on the skerries
of their shipwreck dreams.

AGAINST PROFESSIONAL SECRETS

We'd already been having a miserable time when my father ordered our ingrate of a brother to school. Cured of love, a little late in rainy February, my mother served some yams in the basement. We were seated at the table of my dad and my older brothers. And my mother sat herself down at our feet in the same gesture that a fireplace does, in a house. We touched the door.

'The door's been touched!'—my mother.
'The door's been touched!'—my own mother.
'The door's been touched!'—said all parts of my mother.

Walk on, native daughter, *a* daughter, to see who's shown up this time, said me (sounding yucky like Telemachus).

And, without waiting to see who'd shown up to take the maternal slot, A., my brother, the son who'd left to see the world but now left to see who'd shown up this time, opened the door.

The weather took over my family. Mom got cold and distant. She made it to the patio outside. She was the cold and the distance. If you're picturing clouds right now, you're halfway there.

Then pain and Pavlov's dogs touched their noses to the front door.

'Because I didn't tell you to leave! The door opens! Be native, daughter,' I heard A. tell one of the dogs. His own dog.

This is all to say this is how I came to throw up my middle finger to the distress of the subjunctive, distress of my father, revealing the man I am in pluperfect rain. He could at the drop of a hat turn on the waterworks so that the windows would seem late by the way they shine.

However:

'And tomorrow, in school,' dissertated Dad, magisterially before a public made of his weekend sons.

And so, the law, the cause of the law. And so it was all my life.

[Mom could have maybe cried, with the shame of her own mother. None of us wanted to eat. Would you have been able to keep your appetite in such a circumstance? The lips of Dad seemed culpable for leaving something broken, a final purse that he knew about. In the mouths of brothers, an absorbed migraine of children. The margarine of summer had already melted.

I left that banal house of water, dizzy from the patio. Such a bad visit. A little too much for me this time. I felt neither too far away nor too thinkable, without being brutal. A clock felt like it was lodged in my throat. But really it was an old shawl, one from Mom's drawers, a pattern of chickens on it that hadn't incubated any eggs yet (I took the scarf to wrap around my head because I had a headache, heralding my skill of tying something tight across my temples.) I'd forgotten the incident instantly, the scarf was part of the life of her children. It was cold for the cows and all of the eggs. A clucking lasted after its verb.

No one spoke to me in Hebrew at home, only English. And about wanting to speak to me in more than one tongue, no one left me a sign that it was left in them, a hot-cold meal Mom made.

'Where are the kids of the old chicken?'
'Where are the chickens of the old chicken?'

Poor things. Where could they be.

MY POEMS WON'T CHANGE THE WORLD

It was like
I confused myself with the little house
I was in, looking
to move elsewhere
in the room

Like I was told to
look thru the window
so I did, at a minor red brick
and a branch
I couldn't put my left check on

It was like
so what that the window stopped me
and each branch
was several conscionable diagonals
the window further
divided

It was like
I considered my position
disadvantageous to disarming
the form of my position

It was like
that dull ache passing
for a tooth

SEPTEMBER 30TH, 2005

this is how it starts for us,
the both of us screaming,
your little lungs giving out their very first roar
and me, on the other end of the cord,
left smouldering in the embers
of that temporary madness...

                              and now, all these years later,
                              that cord has been cut,
                              you still have the lungs of a lion,
                              and we are both still screaming.

PATCHOULI

on nights i'd go to see her she'd leave the key to her apartment
for me underneath the green wheelie bin on the gravel out front.
i'd busy myself until she got back, mostly by browsing her dvd
shelf and giving myself a little tour of the place, stroking her many
cats (she had 5). i had no clue about what she'd been doing or where
she'd been, she'd just go around filling the cat bowls with biscuits
and water, and then we'd get down to the business of what i was there
for- watching dvds and fucking. she'd light incense sticks to cover
up the cat shit smell. i can still taste that awful combination in my
mouth now- patchouli and shit- and that was that until the next time i
came over and rummaged around the gravel in the dark for the feel of keys.
i broke it off when i found out what she did for a living, not that i judged
her for it or because i was in any way disgusted, but it's just that when you
grow up as an only child, you are not cut out for sharing your things.

TAYLOR. FUCKING. SWIFT.

thanks to my teenage daughter, if you dare me to sing you
every single song taylor swift has ever written, i could easily
do it, lyric perfect too. in our house taylor's name is sacred,
her face repeated on our walls like the image of our blessed

lady mary, and i feel i ought to make the sign of the cross each
time i pass it, even though i am not a practising catholic. i once
asked my daughter who she would save if we were both drowning,
me or taylor (she could only choose one of us), and i knew

by the awkward silence that followed that it would be me left sinking,
mouth open in a silent scream, while taylor is pulled from the water,
caramel hair falling in perfect, wet curls like an all-american mermaid,
ready to write her next song about heartbreak.

CAPABLE OF TREATING

there was even a time — when I didn't — answer the phone

I would — let it — ring her

voice — reminded me — I was still

alive — and — able to

to access — the descent of the — present

the descent into — the night — into the night of

the night — of non-exposure — exposure

I soaped — his back — I soaped his back

at — the public showers — but it got too crowded

crowded and — when I had to leave — I slipped

scattered — skin touching

imagining — how I — accomodate

for an event to — provide — a condition

generate — my own scaffold — with or without

outside — I become ballast — myself

a spat that gutters me — that gutters me — by othering my legs

my legs — as though they permanently — crossed and somehow

twisted or untrustworthy — queer — means to

to make possible — open swerve connect — embody

curves — organs that unravel via — the subject

capable of treating — some points of the world — occurs

the real — that summons — summon us

to the abruptness of — a decision — or an instrument

of equality — a traced line that misses me — opens

to a new — present — to a new present

thinking now I wonder — is it that the door didn't fit — or was left

FEELINGS ARE FACTS

how do you train
something too
happen
you're the only
happening
these events
fold
seams that connect
in memory
rubbing
stretching to reach
blades
deliver the trees
when art plays
is not as difficult
I go outside
something
to myself
only
when I speak
when you've already
tragic
a door I'm
myself
mirror
a towel
thread in
a knot

desire to enjoy
thick
and you
witness you're
turning back to
events make
folds that
in fragments
that helps
cream
between the shoulders
where
time played a
against another
in my mind
to find something
else that happened
the
makes itself
it out like
you've already stopped

gay I
quietly
sob
inhaling the
trails to my
precariousness

the taste of
a thing can
find
on the other side of it
yourself
ruptures
conceal and seams
establishing rifts
doubt
into my neck
shoulder
can we
part feelings are facts
cultivating the terrain
but for the wind
misremembered
but kept it
mistake only
known
trying to continue
momentum is
a limb through a
whisper to myself
in the
into a
cotton
stomach
tum

NOT RINSING

going

trying to

jaw

takes on a

trying to settle to

thing

pre-emptive

when it is

profound

the palate

runs

rush back in to

to

speak and

heavy and shake the

circularity it

direct

it avoids it has

warnings

grasped

but turgid

of all

around

cover

attempting to

tell makes the

the speaking

runs around

to land on the

clauses

disclaim and

the speech is not

rinsing

hope until the

word

silence

I SWEAR I KNEW NOTHING

No good jokes, no secrets,

no presidents' names,

not what Americans meant

when they said IN THE NAME

OF DEMOCRACY or why there were sheep

hanging upside down in the garage,

not silence, not outrage, not the men

shouting NICE JEANS at me from their cars,

not the number of annual burglaries

in five neighbouring postcodes or words

like postcode, hand job, duck confit,

in a simulated crash the dummy is never

a woman and I didn't know that

either, not yoga or burnout or the thrill

of crossing a small violet line.

Three men climbed on top of a yacht

and waltzed into our apartment.

We couldn't figure out what they'd stolen

but we knew we wanted it back.

THE DETAILS HERE ARE NOT IMPORTANT

maybe there was
a washing machine
on the roof

a cracked pot
of blue jasmine
teetering over
the parapet

I was there
with my big
mouth
pulling up
my wet skirt

the rain came
in ladles which
is not important now

I see them all
the things I should have done

locked the roof garden
twisted and pulled out
each tooth like a tick
yelled about women
and cockpits and pecking

for worms
I should have
said something
better but

if you are wondering
if I waited

                yes,

with the wilt
of an abandoned
tulip I waited
and waited
to be plucked out
of the mulch

for a swamp mouth
to open and call me
a good green thing
worthy of light

April

THRESHOLDS

after mahmoud darwish and bülent ersoy

I

invisible visible

the making before birth

as threshold of identity

absent in its point

bodily transaction

presented in prehistoric

               violence

along the stretch of contemporary

                    freedoms

voice transferred for bleeding

               Presents

II

if halfcut at axis when trauma turn left and coaches stand at operations in check, istanbul futures on bridging scars where wounds cauterise at the half-axial movement, modesty's mistress mistrust interpellative action ready-made already done in-action / daily humdrum urban milieu, sunflower pips, spread of salad, chorba and cacik, chai sipped in ancient action from saucer to lip, traumatic recurrences papered over with lino / rock psych and western garb / neo-europe as post-asia / polyglot returned as de-transitioned exchange / goods revealed orally, pre-auratic stance wrapped in plastic, paper-bag running cherry-tasting / vegan summoning in venture entrepreneurial ethno-business as linen-stripes and faulty light-switches / permeable archipelagic ardour as parabola pasts intersect at disjunctive points — cultural, epistemic, performative — turkic presents, london town fecundity in social breakdown — waking deaths — unmarked problems, urban problems — passive polities, politically rife, resolute insolence, antagonistic elevations — unsuccessful navigations in colony collapses, culinary conditions for ripening palates / aesthetic form distributed inordinate and detached / detailed debasements laundered in high-rise shores / widening paths occidentosis in post-islamicate tomfoolery / verlust at the hole-in-the-wall post-prole pre-capitalist perfidy / performed resignations / i breathe confessional warmth / i eat in essence / in pre-common state / i wish to bodily frame / through the blessed queers / the pre-lingual affectation, the movement of lingual judgement and nominative justice / the face of an-other / one an-other / browning health / sub-porous intent / an ethical recognition / the canteen as relation / the disinterested hospitality as being brought into the fold / choice done away with / bedecked in throes of wonder, guilt, fomo, restlessness looking to us here in content gliding possibility

/   after the event vibes

III

in wakening softening cherry skins,

taut (socratic) growing burdens of speech imposition —

outed inferences in the growing toil —

i was speaking rhetorically —

the conversation kept on non-verbal —

communication continue —

tanning slowly under kitsch suites —

dulling desires, caught in two —

over leisure in multiple desires tanning

consumerist in a bid for connection —

destructuring reminisces as post-nostalgic /

the conversing in absence after *absence* /

a further coming down /

evading a figures placed bodily straight and strict /

machine gun coloured administration in the head

weighing down like the original subalterns /

twisted queer lives — multivalent — street smart *girl* /

weathered woman, service male, petit flaneur,

casualised poet, pre-fabulatory gusto and angst

Desert hills all
aflame   The old hopes
  an oak shook through a screen

Our separate smoke
caught
  in the same ascent   Months
  I move in you

Rosemary
dead   Naomi at the clinic
Leah in hospice in bed
& debt   Throwing a book
to the thresher a poet read
So much less than our
nakedness   a chorus
                a garland
                of changing names

Awaiting

not clarity

but mineral a membrane

              between us stooping

              to rock a woman rises

              armful of color

              of evening

              kelp

so much to learn
about the
Soviet space program

but still:
where did it lead?
to nothing-

ness the likes
of which
we'd only dreamed

before and
yet: here we are
reading in

our library bored
out of our
minds: body lulled

by this ripe summer
mood swelled
up to wash us down

in early 1955 the legal
status of space
still hadn't been defined

so would the Soviets
accept a flyover
by an American satellite?

their not protesting it
would help
establish the precedent

of course they claimed
that all of
this was for peaceful

purposes although
finally it
didn't matter

because Sputnik
beat the Americans
into space

along the western coast
of Ireland
Canadian bodies wash

ashore
are buried nearby
their plane

destroyed by u-boat
fire the
only monuments

to these
men are graves
they rest

all but forgotten
each one of 40
thousand Canadians

who gave their
lives as
part of a moral

obligation
or for other reasons
colonial

SURVIVORS

A green cloud above us, we smoke and laugh
our cares and last night's hangovers away.
Life, frankly, has never seemed so funny.
Penarth beach is a mix of sand and shingle
that stretches below us, as we perch on a cliff top.
The scents of sea air and weed burn our nostrils.
The tide is getting closer. It cuts the beach in half.
The sky grows grey. It'll be evening soon.
'Do you remember last time we got stoned here,
and I persuaded you that island was Majorca!'
My mate, Will, points at some distant flecks of land.
'Yeah, yeah,' I say. 'The tide is coming in fast.
We should make a move.'
'Roll one more up first, mate.'
So, we smoke one more and decide we'll have
our milkshakes and Chilli Sensations in the car.
All we can think about is curing the munchies
as we get off the cliff, using a ladder of rocks
we'd made earlier. We stumble down the beach
and turn a corner. Icy air stifles our laughter.

The tide has reached the top of this part of the beach.
It's lapping against the edge of the cliff
and we don't know any other way out.
'We'll have to climb up the cliff again
to get across,' I tell Will.
But this side of it is too steep. We'd fall to our deaths.
We'll just have to get our feet wet, I suppose.

We've still got the giggles as we tread through the water.
But the waves are hitting us harder than we thought,
and the sea is rising up our bodies now,

smashing us against the base of the cliff.

A wave gives me a wallop and I'm submerged.

I remember what a fortune-teller told my mum:

'Keep your firstborn away from water.'

I raise my head and peer at the sea,

beautiful and terrifying at the same time,

stretching to those ever-distant flecks of land.

I think about the things I haven't achieved

and sob like a child who wants his parents.

You hear about this sort of thing in the news:

fishermen drowning like this.

And that's all Will and I will be remembered as:

two idiotic boys who drowned on Penarth beach.

'Come on!' I shout. I won't let that happen.

I cast my milkshake. It bobs on the water like a gull.

We swim back to shore, gasping for breath,

oblivious to the cramp in our arms and legs.

I want to collapse on the grey pebbles.

But I sprint up the beach, desperate to get away.

Afterwards, we sit in Will's car, drenched.

Somehow, I've managed to save my packet of crisps.

But I can't eat now. I pull my phone from my pocket.

Beep. Beep. A telephonic death rattle.

My wallet, with all my cards in, is soaking.

'Did we just nearly die?' I ask, shivering.

'That was the scariest thing

that has ever happened to me,' Will responds.

Partly ecstatic that we're still alive,

but mainly furious that we were so bloody stupid,

we sit in silence, shaking our heads.

We decide to stay away from each other for a few days.

Like survivors, hoping to forget.

WHEN YOU HELD MY FINGER

on the night our parents brought you home,
i crept into their room while they slept
so i could take another look at you.

you gazed at me with your blue eyes,
studying my face under the moon,
amazed by the world beyond your cot.

i inhaled your newborn scent, ran my fingers
through your tuft of red hair.
you were tiny, soft as the moonlight.

when you held my finger in your palm
i felt something that i won't feel again,
at least not until i become a dad.

and now, you're nearly as tall as me,
and insist that you have more pubic hair
than i do, even though you're just twelve,

but we've stayed close since you held my finger.

FIELD NOTES 2020

I trace the dark pattern of bronchioles in the branches of a March oak. Leaves at its base, dry as a cough, turn in a sharp wind. Spring is locked out save the singing. I open the catch to blackbirds, robins, wrens.

*

The not-so-busy main road is the distance between us; being me and my dog at the entrance to the park on the one side, on the other, the Polish lady who breeds Miniature Pinschers, and for whom I am sometimes mistaken if people look at dogs and not their owners. I wave. She waves back. Her two dogs sniff at something irresistible by the cherry tree; mine is focused on fox scat.

*

My new acquaintance, Ben, from across the road thinks the poor turn out for Thursday night's applause is due to the nature of the people who live around here. He does not elaborate. I'm happy with the quiet. He enjoys daily bike rides on empty streets.

*

Lounging in the park is against the rules. Luckily my favourite place in the world is my bed. It's commodious and my dog is happy there too in his self-made duvet nest. I've read, written and suffered in it for years. Some days it's hard to see the covering under the layers of paper and books. Some days, like the last twenty one, they go untouched. First light is the best light, when the sun streams directly in my window for an hour or so. Miss that and writing in the shadow of my hand is done.

*

I woke to a damp garden: thirsty plants watered, flagstones washed clean and all those stripy pebbles from Wales shining. I may not be able to walk on the beach for many months, yet bands of quartz in weathered grey hold a promise of the waves. And then, a pair of great tits on the feeders.

*

Stratus, stratus, stratus roof the blue as a crow flaps from right to left across my window. The light breeze lifts the newly opened acer leaves. Children in the garden behind are unseen, but content in their play. The sun is just about to disappear behind the tiles. Day twenty three and I am happy in that way when you cannot go into the world. Hostas unfurling. Croziers of fern ditto. Parrot tulips in green and cream with a touch of red are poised to frill about. The boys upstairs are playing funky music. All is right.

*

The late cherries are more profuse than their early cousins; everywhere redoubled: in the little corner park at night, a white glow of petals under street lamps; in the morning a deep pink overflowing Askew Road by the bus stop. Both playgrounds are barred with shiny chains and padlocks. A council worker stands on the back of a pick up to remove the basketball hoops.

*

When the park was closed for a week, I tried to smell gorse flowers on Wimbledon Common. Today I scoured for native bluebells, found only and only a few, Spanish ones. How I'd love to walk a Chiltern beech wood in its bright green and arching carpet of mauve. A simple weekend trip is non-essential travel, so I must live in the memory of the heady scent of blue, my sense of smell returning.

*

The pink moon is not pink: one night silver, the next yellow, but it is larger than at other times and in that sense, super, and in full view on my night walk, where the usual fox is no more surprised to see me than me him. He stares me out, approaches several paces, then brushes back into the shadows. Bare branches are silhouetted by the moon. Super, I want to bark.

*

Shepherds' Bush Green is a plague burial site. This is unconfirmed, but to this day planning permission is denied. You wouldn't want to be the person to find out, even though you know the infection dies with the victim, or soon after, or so they say.

*

Children are rediscovering, or discovering, the pleasures of chalking the pavement with hearts and messages of love for the NHS. Hopscotch has the thrill of the new, but neither the girl nor her mother knows how to play it. I look around for a handy stone. None are at arm's length.

*

Easter Sunday in Home Park: a mute swan is incubating eggs, her nest huge, the new bulrushes around her, her cob gliding on the dew pond; three black carp sporting; sky larks high above always unseen, but well heard; somewhere a woodpecker hammering; and a surprising kestrel hovering in rosy-blue, then pouncing, his mate on her nest in the hollow of a rotten tree, her camouflage perfect against the cream and brown of the oak. And cherry blossom, fat, pink as our bare arms, cooled only by an imaginary splash from the fountains of Long Water, Hampton Court a mile distant and bright in this unexpected April light. No-one is troubled with anything louder than water and birdsong. Aeroplanes and traffic noise are distant in the memory.

*

The Japanese garden in Holland Park is closed for the duration: a disappointment, but not a surprise. The Dutch garden is approaching its peak: hundreds of tulips, dark and light, their little hearts opening in the blaze, and all the white beds are an attraction and a sadness as I know they will be at their best at night and so, unattainable.

HOSTILE ARCHITECTURE

It is no-one's idea of a world. The outer shell is a jigsaw of meteor craters laced with deposits of bone salt, criss-crossed by blood rivers that congeal into reservoirs. Decisions emerge from an ancient mechanism that focuses evening shadow through a network of caverns into an enormous stone abacus, which converts them into raw data. This is then transmitted via birds, skeletal and sepulchre, traversing blurred skyline like the ghosts of snapped fingers, cast into volcanoes and processed into fire, which burns its way across the landscape, leaving prophecies spelled out in ruin and smoulder. The interpreters know they are complicit and will one day be judged. But they have no choice. They must co-operate. They can't afford to make it angry. They know their place.

THE NEW GODS FIND THE PLACE IN A SIGNIFICANTLY WORSE STATE THAN THEY WERE EXPECTING

the tenants are shadows on sand
banquets boiled down to desert
they are all cactus breeze and
shredded scorpion flakes and you
are stalking their mournful dunes
disguised as a mirage of a delicious
refreshing ice-cold beverage

laying yourself out, adopting
the fussy contours of an oasis
the condemned being kneeling
to slurp desperately of blessed
moisture, tongue finding only grit
and bleached bone and your
laughter, pummelling like a
military-grade sandstorm

you are in a foul mood but
cannot seem to articulate why

too many hours chewing through dust
maybe, searching for the source of this
insomnia, too many grizzled sessions
with passing genies, chopping up
burning lines of fire ants just to feel
something, like there's still some *you* left
like this billion-year trip was worth the
hassle, and sure, why not spend the

next billion planting trees, this place
may never be a garden again but you
might as well try while you're here

RAIN DANCE

like parodies of DNA, we feedback,
knotted in uneasy loops, up to our
eyeballs in ocean, shiver-tapping
toes to The Anthropocene Rag. a
benefit concert in a lake of glacier,
bidding for drops of exotic puddle.
raising awareness! gallows humour!
line goes up! we give thanks for our
swollen feet. for overly oxygenated
blood. for the novelty of constant
vertigo. what is collective bargaining
on a beach of molten glass? in a library
of bones? on the moon, looking down,
trying not to think that this new gravity
feels an awful lot like *I told you so*?
we are discussing the formation of a
new crisis committee. our office is
all melt water and microplastic. our
chairperson has never killed an
elephant. our priorities are noble.
item one of one on the agenda: when
the song resets again, we mummify
in dead grass, worm trail and loam,
offer ourselves up to the mycelial
network, and hope that the roots
propose a workable plan in exchange
for this belated, bodily apology. finally
we find something we agree on: there's
something liberating about surrender

May

THE STOREHOUSE OF EARTHLY DATA GOES DEEPER THAN HUMAN RECORDS

As if becoming broad cloth
I lay myself out flat

chin resting on knuckles
to read   up close   the mee maw

of grass, sheep, wool, water.

I want to disappear
          become a husk.

Windblown and weightless

words become seeds, scattered
in the dips and folds of mother
tongue.

     Feral
          as the teasel grows,

scratching at the nap
of the old tales.
          Tearing the threads.

TOWN HAS NO HISTORY EXCEPT IT BE THAT OF THE RISE AND PEACEFUL PROGRESS OF THE WOOLLEN CLOTH TRADE

Limestone is an animal, a bunch of shells and skeletons, raised up from a crowded sea. I mean Archway is a national fact, as in mild and kindly countryside, as in 1834, the year the memorial arch was built. Gateway to a mansion and the only British monument to abolition. Oh irony, but not.

By this I mean there was a time when I didn't know that cashew nuts grow on fruit looking like a hybrid of pepper and squash. File that under *this seems like a hoax, but isn't,* how that fruit fell apart in my hands and stained my shirt yellow as we sped from Kano to Jos in a cab called Freedom and I had it all. As in freedom. I ate it all up.

The archway still stands, tucked away in a corner of a T-junction, the sweep of the drive long gone, as in a memory of confidence now flanked by council houses, a whole new kind of estate. As in right to buy. I mean isn't the past a lesson, not a life sentence.

The perception of being in a long tunnel, bright lights, as in all people, everyone, equal in death. A sense of benign detachment. I mean when I was ten I found out that one day I will die. I crouched behind the sofa in my volcanic body watching the Indians get killed by cowboys — hundreds of them shot with bullets. Except an overwhelming feeling of peaceful.

Archway as in it's complicated. Meaning at the Wesleyan chapel on Acre Street complaints were made about the women getting up petitions. As in suffrage, as in emancipation, as in another great national invention, as in keep quiet about the hunger strikes, force feeding, decency and the King's horse.

Archway as in particular, as in unique in character, as in eccentric. To be removed from the centre, as in exceptional, team games, home ownership, Ordnance Survey, hypocrisy, the royal household, gardening, being quirkily brave, precision as in a lightning bolt that's 30,000 degrees centigrade, or five times hotter than the surface of the sun. My best t-shirt when I was ten had a lightning flash on it and my mum said *lightning never strikes twice,* as in, made me feel special.

Chiaroscuro, meaning the often-dramatic contrast between light and shade in art, is one of the most mispronounced words in, as in stumbled over, as in stammered through, the English language. As in shame gains power from being unspeakable. I mean radical shadow, light as a refusal of shade, as in we contain irreconcilable multitudes, as in satire, consolation, back-lash. Except in 1834, God only freed the children who were under six years old. As in a proud British boast, except History is how we choose the past. I mean time is created by things; it isn't just there waiting for those things to act inside it. As in time is relative, moving more slowly if an object is moving fast, like a taxicab or a rock-hard ball of fossilised shells thrown through a window.

TO DISAPPEAR. TO FALL ASLEEP

The noise of a hammer on a footstep.
    The waning of the bed of a nail. It follows

that I press abdominal to flesh, press my
    stem to the interference of our sleeping

gristle. How to peel the sunburn from
    an apple. How to slaughter a windowpane

for eventide. A single magpie puncturing
    car tyres, a nest shedding itself. Glass

breaking in all directions, a fever of shards
    alighting with conditions. Outwards and

towards the sea with a fear of maritime lore.
    Creating new forgeries, alarms clocks

for invisible dawns. Of reprehensible longitude.
    Of another morning left to its own devices.

—Aaron Kent

A KAPUŐRÖK MEGSZŰNÉSE / HERLIN-BAMLET PART II

I'm sorry, but a fox is better
at public relations and solar
architecture than the shadow
of a comet engulfed in true
meanings of autumnal bonfires.

If I wanted to know about
the phosphorescence of oysters
sipped inside resplendent ballrooms,
I would lavish in the nepotistic
grandeur of their empty shells.

All silent battalions loosen
inside the nest of a heron more
concerned with the arrival of snow.
The potential for beaks to fracture
oceanic maps of a bloodline.

Ordinary sleep is avoidant of
nuclear weapons, and my teeth
are longer than any young pipsqueak
wanting to be outlived. I apologize,
Borbély, but the hierarchies can

only be smashed by the sacrifice
of a coffin rolled across a minefield.
The sniping of all expensive tyres
to burst our children's headaches
foraged from dead tradition.

— Stuart McPherson

V.1

AN AERIAL VIEW OF HELL

2.

You, ferret-faced angel,
think in disturbances.   lying?
Catatonic culture of literatures;
the (wild lynx of the catacombs stands dead.)
                                      ing
            (s)
1 I keep my demon close:
pacifier of listlessness is death,
a corn-strewn attitude distilled in the fields of dis -
of culled, astonished undergrowth -
this is the curled underlip.   snarled?

The large holes are excrescence ,
in the jubilee garden   jubilant
where christ stood, unwept
I see them at the salt lick with him:
a flock of deer, furred on my ~~tongue~~
tongue, under my coat, under my arm
in woodland: in colour: (from behind)?
drawn to ~~the~~ high places
drawn to the dry, high places,
they do die when I breathe out
and in sickness revive.

High on the winter-tableau of the heart ('s winter-tableau?)
where the deer resist my wild prayer
and the lynx disturbs lochans of peat-water
stepping across the limits of water
transpire-mirror, stern-mirror, disturbed mirrors
rippled like water across the hearing eye of the
spirit's ear / listening heart

NEW MOON 12th July, 1961

This moon looks orbital, ashen, even though it is the the sickle of death or arranged
fire. I have no muscle left in my thought. Anticipation breeds like a
foul smell. The light: HARD.

I have been watching her, of course. It is like watching the back of a ghost.
She has a peculiar gift for absorption. Chameleon-like she can take on
her surroundings, sift through them, and at some level, mimic them.
She seems to refract her surroundings, drawing from them. Sometimes she does it
through description, sometimes by pointing things out to me . . . a shell, the stones
. . . but more often she does it through concentration. She sits with something for
a while, a stone maybe, and when she drops it back into the dust, my imprint is
there, flickering over the surface. This is her gift. It saves her from the mediocrity of
apparent indifference.

Now I must wait. The night's contents will be revealed. But I must
have a drink.

NEW MOON 8TH NOVEMBER 1961

The fattest demon was caught here
in the wet high-pitched screams
of water-stabbed beachings. I was taken
to the flensing room in the old whaling station
and made to converse with demons.

Tonight I suspect
the cave.

HOT CHOCOLATES AT THE INN

There is a tattoo parlour next to a funeral home across the street from the inn where
they have two kinds of dairy alternative milks.

We have to leave soon, you tell me,
as we're slightly far from home and you have plans in a couple of hours.

I think, that's fair enough,
but I'm yet to write a poem with a clever quip
on the significance of a tattoo parlour
being next to a funeral home –
how they are both places of permanence and irreversible events
and both contain the potential for flowers and
negative responses from close relatives.

It's probably best that I don't have the time to spell all this out,
but I want to stay for a little longer anyway,
not necessarily because the hot chocolate is good
or because my feet are still a bit sore from the walk here
or because this sofa has a floral design that my
tattoos just so happen to match,
which naturally, makes me think of death
and to get up and leave would mean moving onto
the next thing and the thing after that
then the next thing you know we'll be back here except
on the other side of the street and I'd
actually rather stay here indefinitely,
and pretend that time doesn't exist.

OTHER PEOPLE

are throwing up in the kitchen sink while on the phone to their ex are falling over
while trying to leapfrog
are telling the truth
are being told they should quit drinking
are having two-day hangovers
are tearing their hamstrings
are falling on their faces
are wandering off without telling their mates
are losing their phones
are spray painting FUCK TERFS on the wall
are shagging strangers on the way home
are ranking their housemates from favourite to least to their faces
are punching walls
are kissing their friends
are trying to do the worm
are thinking about their next drink when they're still on their first are kissing strangers
are passing out on doorsteps
are smoking
are throwing up until 4am in their Tinder date's bathroom post-shag
are falling asleep in the bath
are crying
are buying the entire bar
are dying
are throwing up into the Thames next to the boy they fancy
are stealing fur coats
are upsetting their boyfriends
are getting locked out of their rooms
are getting refused entry
are dancing in the middle of winter in the rain
are beefing the bouncer
are climbing towers they can't get down from
are passing out on stranger's sofas
are spitting in other people's faces

are threatening

are mistaking hand sanitiser for lube

are rubbing dicks

are running into traffic

are forgetting

are doing ket

are falling into rose bushes

are performing spells on empty pint glasses

are shouting back at the comedian on stage

are slipping down the stairs

are shagging the guy their friend really likes

are begging

are running through walls

are stealing from behind the bar

are getting in debt

are stumbling home at 15 after two pitchers of cocktails are making out with their fridge

are screaming

are saying they're from Wisconsin when actually they're Irish are becoming best friends with girls in the toilets are kissing people who don't want it

are singing kumbaya

are getting carried by binmen

are having their hair held back

are falling into Drag Queens

are climbing rooftops

are driving cars

are repeating

are hallucinating

are telling everyone to buy them a drink

are saying *I love you* too soon.

WHEN THE SCARECROWS COME, YOU MUST NOT QUESTION WHY

Instead, let them in like old friends,

allow them to hang their ragamuffin coats

and sit at your table on the steadiest chairs.

Let them eat the decent bread

and drink the cider you've been saving.

They may talk amongst themselves in the low hum

of telegraph wires on a hot summer's day,

they may swoop their pumpkin heads,

or unfasten their patchwork smiles,

but you mustn't read too much into it.

Affect an air of absolute self-assurance:

wear a casual blazer, unscrew the jar of pickled onions

like someone who owns many jars of pickled onions.

If one of them looks at you directly, look back

but not too intently; it has been said

that staring into the eyes of a scarecrow

is like peering down the shafts of great wells –

some have been known to slip.

Of course, not everyone knows the way of scarecrows;

some can hear the click of the garden gate

free from the feeling that something inside

is unlatching. Imagine being such a person –

arranging tumblers along a kitchen shelf,

taking the small, clean weight of a whole glass in your hand,

turning each one against the light and simply thinking

yes, this glass is empty, and yes, this one, empty also,

like someone who really believes it.

AND SO, I STARTED TO DRESS UP AS A SHARK

I enjoy my newfound height –
how people hold doors open as I approach them,
and strangers stop me in the street for selfies
asking if they may rest their heads
upon my white, pillowy underbelly.
I wear the suit so often that friends and loved ones
forget I'm in there
and address their comments to the arrow-shaped head
looming just above my own,
making jokes about custard
while jabbing their pink elbows into my side.
I sleep often – deep, thick dreams
in which I'm lying in a field of grass, blades turning
in the breeze, stripes of sunlight over my arms and legs,
while in the undergrowth,
shadows flash, start to circle in.
When I Google sharks, I learn
that they lack the capacity to dream and so
I empty my head of difficult thoughts,
drip by drip. But I keep coming back
to that house party a few weeks ago,
where a girl cut her hand on some glass
the blood trickling down her arm,
and how in the slim moments before the panic,
frenzy tingled up my spine.
How my mouth went dry,
my skin tightened like leather
and in the mirror, for a second,
I caught myself –
a pair of eyes looking out
from the darkness between
row upon row of jagged teeth.

THE WOMAN IN THE MIRROR

I was as astonished as anyone to find the woman on the other side
of the convex mirror, her face so like my own
only aged in the antique glass. At first, I found her disregard
for my usual routines refreshing: fresh sheets and polished brass,
the apples cut into segments, the nightly urge to light a candle.
She didn't need to plump up her life like an over-stuffed cushion,
instead, she sat in her easy chair letting the days pass through
the house like a breeze from an open window.
But soon things changed. I arranged the spring flowers in a tall vase
only to see the same vase in the mirror with nothing inside it –
save a pool of musty water and a grey, clinging stench.
Friends would come over for dinner and we would drink cold beers
and talk, while the woman in the mirror laughed, animatedly,
to a room with no one in it. One evening, when I was brushing
my teeth, as normal, I caught her pressing her mouth against the glass
and pulling out a large yellow tooth, tossing it in the sink
into a pile of other loose teeth, shining like spare pennies.
After that I couldn't bear the sight of her –
the broad, empty smile spreading over her face.
I wanted to wipe her away, as you might a dirty mark,
or, in more exasperated moments, I even considered taking a hammer
and smashing the glass across the rug.
Instead, I got rid of the mirror, placing it outside
with the old clothes and broken furniture
hoping a passerby would take it far away.
All that remained was a faded, gaping circle on the wallpaper
which is still there, although I'm a much older woman
and it's been many years since I've seen the woman in the mirror,
I wonder if she'd even recognise me now,
what she'd make of what I've become
of my life and of the terrible mess I've made,
and keep making, of it all.

OPEN TABS ON A LAPTOP, 2.38AM

Can insomnia kill you? | Therapy.org

How to fall asleep in 10, 20 or 60 seconds | healthline.com

Rachel (@racheyface) | Instagram.com

How much should millennials have saved by age 30? | Forbes.com

When is a Headache a Sign of a Brain Tumor? | blog.dana-farber.com

Rachel Stone | Facebook.com

Rachel Stone | LinkedIn.com

Rachel Stone (@rachinyourface) | Tiktok.com

Rachel Stone | @therachplace | Pinterest.com

How to get over an ex: 10+ ways to get your life back on track | eharmony.com

What to do if you accidentally like someone's pic | joeblog.co.uk

Online dating advice: 11 ways to win at Tinder | metro.co.uk

How to mine Bitcoin: Everything you need to know | cointelegraph.com

What is the "Free Britney" movement? | harpersbazaar.com

7 Small ways to improve your relationship with your Mom | mindbodygreen.com

Rachel (@rachplaceforever) | Twitter.com

Can insomnia kill you? | Therapy.org

Tall quiet blondes | YouPorn.com

I DON'T LEAK I FLOOD

Yesterday, on a date, I tore off my face.
There are many ways, wet slap of blood on thrusted cunt,
to make arterial splatter. White sheets are clichéd,

but there I was, standing in his miniature bathroom,
foaming up hand soap, scrubbing his sheets, face dripping. Blood
forms a brown cloud-edge, the beginning of a stain. I'd wrecked

my face, tore strips of nose, shredded cheeks, splayed chunks
of breast and pubic hair across his half-sized bed. I hate it when
people don't hang up their towels, that musty stench.

Then, of course, I was worried about his sheets. Congealed
vulva lips and all the multitudinous ways that a liquid leak
is not okay. Fortunately, I am a well-trained woman.

When rage boils and my body explodes, shrieks of shredded skin
under a fingernail's dark trail, I know all about cold water
and the properties of soap. I have scrubbed my face

from many duvet sets, rinsed out bio-matter shards of shame,
cleaned myself from the splattered blast zone.
And here is his sheet, ready for the next. White again.

(POLY)GRAMMATICAL GYMNASTICS

you is a useful term because it is singular and plural
they is a useful term because it is singular and plural

    for the sake of two teas and a coffee on Sunday morning
    for the sake of three croissants and happier than I'd felt in years

say *you* in Russian / say *they* in Croatian / say *us* and say
almost nothing, an almost unnoticeable something

    for the sake of a sentence, for the end-of-meeting chat
    for the sake of clients, for the sake of simplicity

girlfriend was easier at work (also true / also not true)
deeply closeted but slightly closer to saying something

    for the sake of not drawing a triangle and a T shape on a napkin
    and getting into the history of multiplicity

couldn't say *they* with *you* (felt like stealing) quietly tucked away
presenting differently everywhere we went

    it's a bit like coming out as gay ten years ago, isn't it
    maybe it'll be more normal in future

perhaps all my love letters to you are inherently confused
inherently a *you* that is not accommodated by our language

    for the sake of being, for the sake of not having to explain
    some days it's just harder to take up space

June

EASTER

That time they crucified you
but no one showed up –
couldn't work the Eventbrite website,
ignored the invitation on Threads,
didn't pick up the flyer in the café
or see the small ad in the park
pinned up next to English lessons,
hot-yoga tasters, karmic realignment.

SHARD HEART

Piano piano.
Renzo unto Caesar the things which are Caesar's.
Palace in the air.

The Shard is hard to disregard
and this intrepid Reynard
heard about the penthouse chicken coops
and trotted to Floor 72
to stage a feathery coup.

Renzo, Renzo,
Che ne pensi?

You really put the Shard among the pigeons.
Whose nest gets feathered in all this contrail weather?

You've got to pick a penthouse or two,
boys,
you've got to pick a penthouse

                    or two

                          you've ...

got to pick a penthouse or two.

Che ne penis?
Sometimes a Shard is just a shard.

LA GENÈSE DE M. HULOT (POUR JACQUES)

Tati dit: Que la lumière soit! Et la lumière fut.
The Big Bang, as we know,

didn't bang and wasn't big,

but flowered from infinitesimal

to a good thumb-sized pipeful

in the blink of an unevolved eye;

and we know that on the fifth day

Jacques made the fowl that fly

above the earth, and played them

like a theremin with the sun

(which he'd made earlier)

to sweeten the air with song;

and for the sake of divine comedy

he dubbed the sound on afterwards,

and fashioned then the human ear

for the click of rapid heel on floor,

the silent-slamming door, the gadgetry

of tragicomedy, the *rhubarb*

of a babbling Babel; and so began

his gallant dance, the fingertip on satin strap

so as not to stroke the tender back,

so as not to intervene.

MAZORRA

en el pabellón rojo los enfermos
pendientes de la voz como una espada
deletrean la palabra astrolabio
la nada no interrumpe

su discurso borbota de las tumbas
orejas de la muerte
a la sombra rebelde de una ceiba
su voluntad hidráulica

el agua no sigue un solo camino
el sol sabe que se marchitará
por eso en la miseria resplandece

una fuerza verde impulsa la elipsis
la muerte es muda
                        el crisantemo habla por ti

MAZORRA

in the red wing the unwell
awaiting the voice like a sword
spell out the word astrolabe
nothingness does not disturb

its discourse bubbles up from the graves
death ears
in the rebellious shade of a ceiba
its hydraulic will

water does not follow just one path
sun knows it will wither
and so in misery it shines

a green force propels the ellipsis
death is mute
                    chrysanthemum speaks for you

SANTA MARÍA

sin media luz donde caerse muerto
tirado en esta playa
como el cangrejo que no tuvo suerte
y el niño perdonó

compadeces a la piedra que te guiña un ojo
su fresca militancia
y la bicicleta cargada de caracoles
te cruza entre las muelas

la arena en las cesuras
hace que las claves no estén en tiempo
el mundo es una güira pintada como quiera

para la discreción de los turistas
nadie te contó antes
lo que se aprende si sales del agua

SANTA MARÍA

no halflight to drop dead under
sprawled on this beach
like the crab luckless
and forgiven by the child

you feel for the stone that winks at you
its fresh militancy
and the bicycle chock full of seashells
crosses you between claws

sand in caesuras
puts claves offbeat
the world is a güiro painted any which way

at the discretion of the tourists
nobody told you before
what you learn if you leave the water

LET THE POETS LIE

Some things live on in memory
and I want my memories preserved.
        I mean passed down, mouth to ear, to mouth.
        Yes, I've heard of telephone & that's partially the point
just because something has passed
doesn't mean it's not still subject
        to transformation. Take desire, because this is a poem:
        it passes, transforms into what it will— soul love
disdain, boredom, sorrow. The flame
flickers in whispers, tongue to lobe
        tells what it likes, what lies it loves, what it constructs.
        You & I, the old story: we weave it into what we need.

MENAI SUSPENSION BRIDGE

I can't look
down can't even
look at this bridge
today. I'm tired
of the crushing fatigue
that comes over me
when I flee from something
I fear— a flight, the Menai
Suspension Bridge, whatever

it's the suspension part
I think, the long run of road
hanging above the open
water but also it's the height
it's the hanging height of
this sickening bridge. I want
to go to the island, I want to
cartwheel across every danger
but it's not always easy

today I lost the thread and
felt everything close a holloway
falling into itself akin to
agoraphobia

Agor is Welsh for open
it comes from an older word for fence
which is the etymology of Bangor
an ancient city built out from
a fence said the man volunteering
at the cathedral and yes maybe
that's why I feel at home here
in agor's opposite

TWO FOR JOY

"Pitched past pitch of grief / more pangs will, schooled at forepangs / wilder wring."
— Gerard Manley Hopkins

my path led down to the sea to a rocky crop of kelp and scree
sand, glass looking out at the harbour here and there dinghys dotted the seascape

then the path became a tangle of footfalls an amble & I, magpie, pica pica, taking
photos, felt a poem wend and well within me & wham! *Shirley*

inscribed on the seawall & clear as day *she's here she's here I've found her*
& then looking away one single boat moored nearby smacks smartly of Nick

they're here they're here they've found me I have never felt more sure of life
after death nor more held 5,000 miles from home from their graves

his in the sea, hers just at the shore & they are with me holding me close keeping me
safe, as they always did, no, *saving me*, again from my sorrows & solitude

& I, magpie, pica pica, joined by their company (one for sorrow, two for joy)
scrambled around, watering the rocks and gathering a pocketful of tokens

some glass, a shell, some slate, a rusted hinge, a coil of wire brought them home
the trinkets yes adorn my nest but also this new sense— firm substance of absence.

HORSE NATIONS

The only light in this valley
comes from our bathroom
where we've shared water
now stand on the oak chest
four of us in towels in a line
with Dad, a horse yelling
bedtime! I dig spurs into ribs
canter the corridor
jump fallen eucalypts
>   *jump fallen bodies*
>   *I don't yet know are there*
swim rapids, hoof it down cliffs
on a dun national symbol like
'Man from Snowy River'
>   *(poem & film with one white fallen body*
>   *(& if Paterson's lead was Indigenous*
>   *'The Brumby Wars' is on its haunches*
>   *with pros: SEE, MYTH FOR EVERYONE!*
>   *& nos: BUT THE SCREAMING LAND!))*
then exhausted at the station
Dad bucks me into bed, gallops off
rebirths into a black swan
that glides my sister to sleep
in a room with eroded walls.

Plankton farts detected on an alien planet
was the subject line of an email today.
Planet was K2-something. Its surface
covered in water, perhaps.

I turned on a tap to make this rooibos
& water poured out, into the kettle
which shook as I sent messages
prepped the pot.

If we make water go somewhere it wasn't, do we create thirst in the desert?
There are wars in my phone where I order more of what water helped make.

I'll imbibe & go to the beach, watch the dog
watch the statue of C.Y. O'Connor on a horse
barnacles a-bling with the sucked-out tide
cormorant on his head.

Mum calls about a collective present for my 2 y/o niece
but I'm in debt fucking up my home, assuming you all
want to fix things too – & for the life of me I can't
figure out what to buy to stop these endings.

Atoms – yours are mine, Remember?[1]
To wipe cement dust from tiny cheeks, find mothers –

Will we war in slow motion on our new earth?
I'm thinking of astronauts.
The futures we let –
The futures –

There's a graveyard for wind turbines
a Chuck Berry record on the moon & Ayva
up to her chin in Indian ocean, whimpering
at shit-covered bronze.

Not even the past isn't moving –
Read this –   *See?*

After a swim
absurdity in the shower
            washing salt
from my living arms.

HEART

A boxing glove, I can tell you, will never expose
the essential matter of a cheek. Not the blood

or mother who waited in her car, but the decision,
minutes ago, to lace up gloves. A sledgehammer

failed to find this conviction in the walls
of my house. You opened my cheek, found

what? They say there's a firefly below a cup
at the centre of the earth, lighting the glass

like a secret. Could you pick up that cup?
What will you tell my mother, still waiting

in her car, when she learns it's our fault
all the streetlights have gone out?

WHEN WARRINGTON WENT LOOKING FOR FRAMPTON

from the bell,
a blizzard to his head as thuds hissed

on swung gloves, dazed
I realised I was never a boxer. Never a boy

to hit jaws how he hits pads, heart
like Frampton who fires back from the ropes,

defiant.
There's a place for me in their gyms

at a bag,
shadowboxing far from their roped arena

by a mirror,
seasoning my physique with the idea of combat.

While boys slug it out, I work a body of air,
alone

to learn nothing
of how, after hooks crunch a cheekbone

pain thaws
to Frampton surviving the twelfth,

Warrington cradling his leaking forehead
with huge mitts,

ref gathering both fighters in his arms
like the remains of a brood.

TONIGHT I WANT TO LIVE AND

I am trying my best but still the evening trees are printed against the darkening blue

I want so much life from this city but every time I absorb this scene I feel ashamed

how many would kill for this darkening blue

how many have it and don't notice

how many want me to come into their lives

not me exactly but the idea of someone like me

how many have the idea of my life

tonight with its rain on the patio in the porch light

each drop as brief as the time I have with the moss on the brick wall

with the withered leaves that continue to scatter about the road

THE LAST FARE COLLECTOR OF HIROSHIMA

They found her fingers in a jelly of yen

her skin one with the standard issue fare bag

a dove in a sen of silver to go to the mountains oh if only she went.

I have read of a woman who cooled her burns with figs and persimmon

she pared away old skin for years the finest paper it was

writing its kanji into the papyrus sky I wish I knew her.

In the ritual of tea-making I learnt how to sip from a widow's eyes and

learn that some stories are like Hiroshima streetcars

they always arrive on time then the hour takes them.

They found her fables in the evening crow

hopping by the river it is time to hear how atoms sound

when another survivor dies their story sinks at the shore of their eyes.

I have read of a god-fearing woman who feared man so much more

she sliced a cucumber each night for years to cool her skin

and hate had left her years ago with five generations of

Fisherman

    horse-breaker

        cleaner

            librarian

                Mother

                    Father

                        Sister

                            fare-collector.

DEAR MR OPPENHEIMER

Beneath your crafted nebula
I picture your dead noon walk
casting a long shadow eastward.

In the post atomic abendrot
you brush off Alamogordo sand
like glitter from a forbidden kiss.

Dear Mr Oppenheimer,
sky is badged in yellow stars,
magenta stars, violet dust.

Dear Mr Oppenheimer,
this night your star was born
sunset bled over Hiroshima.

At the IMAX film of your life
a man scoffs bulb warm Dorito's
sharing his awe on TikTok –
the new age Brittanica.

TO FEED A NAGASAKI STARLING

She said don't go to the shadows without water —
I have tried to erase him for sixty-four years
and my wrists are tired;
I have scrubbed the darkness of my son
so he could be buried at last in sunlight.

Don't go to my son without removing your shoes —
I have tried to bathe him with prayers and carbolic
but he only gets blacker;
I have lived for ninety-nine years
and starlings are beginning to land by my feet.

Don't wind the paralysed clock,
it is rebuilding the world with seared hands –
I have tried to turn back time
but God will not allow it in Nagasaki;
I had tried to make another child but gave birth to pink curd.

Don't tell them my name,
and look me in the face when you see him —
I have tried to understand
why ink is only spilled by vaporised kin;
I have tried to write a haiku
for the willow which strokes my son.

Don't disturb my son
when the raven plays in the shape of his spectre —
I have tried to shoo it away and it quarrels with my broomstick;
I have tried to tell my son that he was ten yards from living.

I have tried to feed a Nagasaki starling
when it drank the black rain;
I have tried to get it to sing so this wraith could be comforted –
don't disturb my grave and desecrate me
with twitching shadows.

July

EVERYONE IS

You are there, my shape,
my table-daughter, my thorn.
The old conjuror had it wrong.
Something familiar if not memory
lingers in the polished wood.
Who dares ask: are you seen
by the roses in bloom?
Do they peer into your pain
like editors to the edited?
Twist their mouths in hollows
while you become landscape, tree,
a pick to chip at the prize ground
now everyone is dead & gone?

I ASK

Island, what would outdo you for blueness, I ask.
River runs, the bonny zigzags. Thumbnail Alps, I ask.

A non-native of water I am fished to a gin-clear
syllabary by speckled others. Word-blind, I ask.

Street gangs worry at a sense, ah the shambling pine.
Houseflies in radical departure board choppers. Tickets, I ask.

Summer bends, Autumn returns to you, unbidden.
The window panes gleam, dark fangs half-smiling, I ask.

Stone lyre, you are too close for me to dream you.
Who would carve his name in a country without words, I ask.

The heart is also mute, the visible electric steam.
Limited to its own form, a valve opens, a valve shuts. I ask.

A sorry regime's ear catches the shredding of wills.
Love's ablaze, is this a house that cannot shake the fire, I ask.

The exigent Spanish poet wrote verse sweetened
By tender advice bright with lemons; what sense is this, I ask.

Staccato raindrops head south. Gravity or
The call of the great silver factory. A cup of water, I ask.

Paris or Bologna, the scholastic's wintry dilemma.
Needlework or a quiet night sitting in front of the telly, I ask.

Bach's nocturnal crepitations, a pluvial sarabande.
O Universe, why do we wait for night for you to fix, I ask.

If time is a homeland, remember me before I existed.
Island, let me rival you for love, age happy, with no sad drumbeat, I ask.

SNOW BUDDHA

Time never lay so heavy
As the snow that made
                    you

White-mouthed
Letter-boxed
                    mouthed
Addressee
Of our old
                    selfhoods

So what's the story
Are we really
                    cool witnesses
To our own vibrations

Is that it

How wonderful
& sad

Half of me was expecting
                    more

SUITCASE (EVERYTHING, EVERYTHING WILL BE ALRIGHT, ALRIGHT)
after Hanif Abdurraqib

You turn up with a box of Double Brown, tears running through your teenage stubble, turning the cardboard to mush, snot caking your Planet 8 hoodie and 1st XV stubbies, the stale malt forming an unholy union with Lynx Africa, and you told me your parents couldn't see themselves in each other anymore so they're separating and you no longer believed in permanence and *why would they do this*, on the eve of our final match, *why would they do this,* because what's a team without a captain and what's a captain with a lip that rattles like an empty can and shoulders that refuse the load, and the beer was so warm when we opened it, why was it so warm.

You said your dad wouldn't look at your mum when they told you, and your sister kicked the PlayStation so hard the disk holder jammed and you couldn't retrieve Tony Hawk's Underground 2 (your favourite game), even though rugby boys shouldn't skate, but I think you liked the idea that maybe you could if people stopped strapping orphaned hope to your name, or maybe you just liked the soundtrack, soaring over abandoned warehouses and aircraft hangers to *Joy Division* and *Jimmy Eat World,* slicing through pavement pixels so fast all the surroundings knit themselves back into static and you on your board floating, suspended, spinning.

But I didn't have that game and I didn't know what it was like when the old gods disappear and your house of worship gives way to sand, I just watched as you whispered into the can *don't tell the boys for God's sake don't tell the boys.*

In our hometown, a box of Double Brown is called a suitcase because it will always take you on some regrettable journey, and like the one you found half-packed in your hallway that morning, the fear and uncertainty a suitcase carries can leave any promised destination in ruin.

Until that day I'd never held someone who was both boy and man at the same time and your fingers scratched a word into my ribs that looked kind of like brother, and lover, and friend, all at once. But nothing in this life is more reckless and hopeful than interpretation.

When Tony Hawk became the first person to land a 900 he said that during the final spin he existed in his own orbit and that up there nothing could touch him, not even the dirt, but the dirt was all we had, how could we be so in debt to the engineered physics, because in that room it all became static, and why was the beer warmer than our hands pressed together, and can we still see the words we scratched into each other, even if they aren't really there like phantom limbs, and who does the memory speak to now the simulation has disappeared, *don't tell the boys for God's sake don't tell the boys.*

GOOD KIWI LAD
after sam sax

Lives in his own shadow
with his own hands and many others
finding home around his neck because
he was told to play rough and listened
to his mate who said his old man
would kick him out the house if he was
or at least if he ever found out
so he waits for captain's orders
like the good shepherd Moses
that insufferable nerd trying
not to doubt the grizzled flame
us boys can swallow anything
with these inherited stomachs
our organs don't regenerate they're trained
and lashed until they can't learn anymore
like a spent mutt who can't muster
bark or bite so he hides behind past toil
because nobody should take it easy nobody
should lie in the soft wreckage of comfort
should dream of tongue in old mate's throat
in the woolshed at dusk when the missus is
sleeping but she'll be right and he'll be wrong
and wrong again sometimes it just happens
rising like a shitty tide like acid reflux
that fills the heart but doesn't stop it
he'll swallow some more and keep it down
like the myth of Sisyphus except sadder
because he is the rock and he is the mountain
and he is the deception and he is nobody
and no body and nobody defies the gods.

OH SMALL PSYCHIC BIRDHOUSE

let me in!
I am weary of human
failed molars & fish-ball soup vision

black drop of basalt
I too am mineral
forgive me a sigh
is a word for repentance

midsummer casts me home
standing as I will in your hall
waiting for ticking
shade to align

insects and pips drop
I'll break false wings
to touch your cool structure
rest a while far from influence

let me in let me in
I will peck all night
and then some
until blood matts feather

[Invocation to rescued sculpture on Space Station 1]

Outside, all through the assigned night, machines drone against the silence – creating tiny tracts of light, stitching rhythm into the soft lapse of space. I'm here at the sculpture again whilst others shut their eyes, a reclamation of sorts, a tiny rebellion. I am compelled to be in its proximity although touching is forbidden. I feel particles of igneous bounce against my face. I can smell ions. I write.

She was revered, the sculptor. A female who worked with psyche and trauma – creating architectures of witness and resistance. My own avatar is a blackbird, one which protects its nest, slides down icy grooves for fun and takes in all the snowy peaks reflected in its amber eye. Eats worms. The blackbird is not *cruel* as the word does not exist for it, only survival exists. In this form I can write. I know that birds did not write but birds were true bird whereas human was false. And out of this, writing and other things emerge. The surface is shined by lyric and I am reflected in this. Half bird and then half not. If there had not been mirrors would we all be saved? What is the power of attention?

— *Archivist*

THE FLAMINGO GUESTHOUSE

"Log phase –
growth is exponential
& therefore time is dead"

Frank! Remember the days
we got wasted in Miami?
Where we'd drink, be wild

hold faith in the sea bed,
eat like kings of old!
Why did we do it – open

to destruction at every turn?
What I'm arriving at is
modern reality is an exclusion zone.

We are beyond ill,
yet still write beautiful reviews
on human behaviour! Man...

Standing on window ledges
is exhausting.
The big question,

will we make the changes
in time?
We have to succeed, Frank.

Block chain rewards are hot,
locations of ice, rare,
the earth crew are fragile

compared with us up here.
We know it may be too late.
[A robot takes Jim's order]

~Let's start with black lobster substitute &
plant-based cream? ~
I'm fresh out of ideas, Frank.

1.   Sleep, work, bed, he is saying, standing in the heat
     on the turn of the winding path where we run, standing
     with a woman whose hands pat her hijab as she listens,
     offering to it what she cannot give him, as he tells
     what each day holds now, sleep, work, bed: nom, cheghel, takhet,
     as if sleep and bed are different states (and they are),
     one what comes eventually, one the place we go to wait
     till it does, sweating humid on July nights, in an electricless
     Lebanon: neither fans nor AC, bed an interminable site
     of waiting to see whether sleep will come before tomorrow,
     breathing into fug's thick warmth, body wearing ways
     it would never have chosen when, as a child, it dreamt
     of what would come, sleep, work, bed, in a stateless
     Lebanon, where mercy is how eventually bed turns to sleep

2.   sleep, work, bed: yes, how we put our body in places
    where nothing happens, places for signs and wonders,
    and nothing happens, only echoes and waiting, what
    passes is only time, what grows is weariness and age,
    what goes on is endurance; and the things place is made for
    are wistful dreams, growing quieter, growing harsher,
    more crude and grasping, crave of sleep, darkening
    hunger, frantic sex frustrated for release, body wasting
    while it waits and hope concatenating into urgent fantasies
    to hide shamefully in the morning: I go to bed to wait
    for sleep, he is not saying, sleep does not come, only
    onslaught and worry, he is not saying, and she listens,
    thinking — imagine it — how bodies & places & happenings
    are meant to meet and how, when they do not, we drift, a fluke

1. fluke in the light, drifting, she might be thinking,
    or how a life passes waiting for things to resolve
    themselves, waiting for real life to begin, or living
    (as she has heard him say) on the edge of real life
    knowing this is it   & now he is saying yesterday
    for four hours he was queueing on a highway waiting
    for petrol, and he had more luck than his neighbour
    who slept there in his car overnight   even the rich,
    he is saying, even those with a backlog of cash-crisp
    savings or supply of dollars fresh enough to hold value
    are having to queue and so they pay someone with time
    on his hands   (so many workless men) time enough
    to sit in the car   (so many workless men) inch forward
    schwe schwe by the hour   it's a job as good as another

at the riverside retail park

inside poundland

under the swinging banner of aisle three

we could share

a hotdog in the april dusk

outside the sun, a prick of blood

swimming in a purple sky–

the colour of your knuckles clenched

during a fasting cbc

your fist clutching

my ketchup'ed pinky

the refrigerator staring back at us,

baring open its cured meat smile

our everyday

squabbling   haggling

butchering   budgeting

in retail aisles. a lick of mustard

at your mouth's end. i want to french you like

alain delon in *plein soleil*. **WE COULD COOK**

MEATBALLS FOR DINNER, we could leave

the delhi metro behind–

we could do taxes on an excel sheet

make 2-for-1 grocery lists

ration our rice.

we could drink a hellish drip

at some hellish café. sunday mornings.

toothpaste kiss.

do you think we could have had that life?

the human hippocampus is responsible for our memory, dreams, and imagination. i think we took our temporal lobe and called it love. we made a house in there. the bricolage came and stuffed it with birdsong. i filled it with thunderstorms. my fists full with childhood. the house of my brain, a vineyard of windchimes. the hippocampus drunk on the very first firsts.

memory, dreams, imagination are interchangeable.
dreams are an interlude. they are parentheses. an afterthought in articulation.

an octopus changes colour while it dreams in its sleep, turning canary from ivory, pulsating like a lighthouse underwater. and i wonder: if the best of us show our true colours when we spell out our dreams too.

the etymology of 'dream' roots it in *deception*, meaning: the very nature of a dream is to be false. in my dreams, thus, even you can't live up to the idea of you. call it imagination. **the realm of the hippocampus.**

i dream of you – is this ambition?

if ambition is desire, then wanting you is an enterprise. a full time job. a labour of hubris.

(ambition is arrogance. but so is love.)

i want you. is desire greed?

i want to tell myself i am better than this, better than the foolish tantrums of my heart.

i clutch the gore of summer in my hands, the rot of youth between my teeth.
i have no city i can leave behind.
i have no room where this desire can be a tenant; so, it lives in me and unfurls in my stomach like a child i will never have.
(the word hippocampus comes from the greek word for a seahorse.
what i mean is: i am a single parent to this longing.)

to me, you are the sum of my desire, destiny, destination.

i want you, because wanting you is the easiest thing i have ever done.

i want you beyond audacity, beyond the indignity of desire.

i want you. is desire good?

(in my dreams, i trace the feverfew moles on the nape of your neck. nobody is in a hurry to wake up. the morning is fresh linen, it rains soda pop outside; all our windows, blurred, a fizz. the bed is our enterprise of love. we stay in because we want to.

we stay in because nobody needs to exit the hippocampus.)

THE INTERVIEW

She sat in the office waiting room, picking her nose and eating it. Her jeans were dirty. She could smell herself. A poster opposite urged her to take out a life insurance policy. She tore it down and built a fire in the wastebasket to warm her hands. The secretary remembered something he had to do, took his coat from the stand and went out. A gust of cold air whipped round the room, disturbing papers and causing the filing cabinet to fall on its side. As it fell, drawers slid open revealing reams of carefully filed papers. The ceiling fan spun into life. The light on the CCTV camera flashed. It must be summer by now, she thought. She took off her jeans and hung them over the curtain rail by the open window. Outside the office, the heat was record-breaking. Her cab driver sweltered in the taxi, engine idling. *Wait*, she'd said. *How long will you be?* he'd asked. *I don't know, just wait*, she'd said again, pressing a hand to his cheek.

SWORDS

Later, she found it. It was titled, 'The Sword'. She'd screwed it up into a tight little ball and swallowed it. It had taken a minor, self-administered surgical procedure to retrieve it from her digestive tract. As she looked at it now, partially digested, spotted with blood and stomach acid, she wondered if the party had been worth it after all.

The following day, she visited the museum where 'The Sword' was being held. On the roads, traffic slumped lethargically. She passed between the columns of the grand entrance and enquired as to the exhibition's whereabouts. When she first entered the space, she was bemused. The museum had carefully unfurled 'The Sword' and attached it, she knew not how, to a piece of wood, then hung it on the wall. There were some people standing around in silence, staring at it. Afterwards, she visited a local café and asked for a sandwich.

August

1.

In skin under sun batons
Fall like night across your face.

It's spicy on the streets this evening
Pulled into a car they say who

Are you, dissembled into flesh unmade
By siren song & bullet pocks

Upon the shell of what is named
When cops speak — the sound

Of glass irrupting, its laughter track
Of burning in reverse, as choppers shred

Night to sheets that settle on the lake
& melt as dawn interpellates the shadows,

Now fucking answer.

6.

Where the shoreline meets the forest meets the rent
Burden, about sleep the landlords are getting unruly
At the mouth here I'll place this mask for you gently

Your body like a land mass leaving the world behind
For whatever that ocean & all its flames might want to say
To you as gulping down the violence you chose. Our

Salary wrapped in plastic around your death, ventilated
In the brutal morning of grass climbing its slight persistent grasp
Around the pillar once they called a spine, an economy

Of coughs trickling down, like piss, like a lover dying again
In your tired arms, that you sent into the murky checks & balances
Of guttural sky, that open bruise, that premonition of a better ghost

To come & haunt you. This is how it looks to watch your family
Die, that they had no choice, that your living tongue moves
In them, as they tend the lawn & reluctant lungs abate

The noise of what it felt like just to be you. We pin that badge
Of your silken face in freezer, slick upon thaw, a stray dog
Chasing down the warmth at the end of fear, at the end

Of the sentence curdling down your chin, the pool of flames
At your feet polished our back into fresher air, the flicked skin
Skimming like blustered cloud on blue from night collapsed.

KING CURTIS

In the shop the sweets spill on the floor
you have cried a thousand times, imagining life
made out with, lonely blimp of my heart
be bashful in the glare of sweeping lights
on the street where feeding failed. They all want
to eat the sweets, in the centrefold of the city
staring back with basic infinite love
display cramming its mouth down the middle
to never be entered. You cannot have my bacon
you will die but that's why I need it, the songs
are repeatable life & that can't anymore portray
satisfaction. Withdrawal of love is the death of you
I pray for in sincerity every day, just to eat
in the comfort of being a person, chasing
you down, every single sweet that stands its ground to bask
enlightened in the certainty of being scooped back up.

RÓJKA: STRUKTURA RUCHÓW

po ojca przychodzi ten spod lasu (ten co topi
w mule rzeki wszystkie suki rodzące się w oborze)
mówi że ciemna masa obsiadła wejście chałupy

na miejscu zastajemy potężny rój który wciska się
w szpary pod progiem

ojciec kropi go zimną wodą rój cichnie odnajdujemy
królową i przenosimy jej kruche ciało do wiklinowego
kosza *musisz być czuła ruchy niech będą powolne*

matkę otaczają pozostałe pszczoły zanosimy je
do chłodnej piwnicy ojciec przygotowuje ul dadanta
na ich przyjęcie w tym czasie wielokrotnie schodzę
do ciemnego wnętrza i słucham

SWARMING: STRUCTURE OF THE MOVES

father is visited by the neighbour (the one who drowns
in the river silt all the bitches born in our barn)
dark matter swallowed the doorway to his house

we discover a giant swarm squeezing inwards
through the cracks under the threshold

father sprinkles the swarm with cold water it falls silent
we find the queen and transfer her fragile body
to a wicker basket *you must be tender your moves must be slow*

the worker bees circle the mother we carry them
to the cold cellar father prepares a nucleus box
for their homecoming i often go down
to the dark interior and listen

MATKA BOSKA: GIPSOWY KLEJ

wynosimy ją na werandę mamy tam dobre światło
jej głowa rozłamała się na wysokości ust *żeby jaka*
kara boska za to na was nie przyszła

sklejamy matkę boską od dołu szukam odłamków z wężem
potem stóp naskórek dłoni twardnieje od schnącego kleju
ostatecznie matka boska wygląda przyzwoicie brakuje
jej tylko serca i w plecach ma dziurę to tam będę wrzucać
ciężkie monety wykradane z niedzielnego płaszcza ojca

MOTHER OF GOD: PLASTER GLUE

we take her out to the porch the light here is good
her head split at her lips *god forbid*
calamity it may bring

we glue mother of god from toes up i look for the snake
bits feet the skin of my fingers hardens with the drying glue
finally mother of god looks decent she lacks only
her heart and in her back there's a hole where i will drop
heavy coins stolen from father's sunday coat

RIFLE

we have begun a game of forty forty, unaware,
dirty thirty standing, unmoved but armed. tea ladies
threaten. dawn chorus clanging. tap tap on a rifle

as we stifle laughs. this is for you and you. cheeky chappy
trigger-happy. forty forty i see joan connolly behind the tree
each pop will stop mammy in her tracks. forty forty save me

because we aren't going back. sing song where's your
mother gone. dispatcher body-snatcher. all night long in
the scratcher. ping pong bing bong i'm not wrong. tag, you're it.

STRAY BULLET

Bullets roam the streets in packs observing. One breaks away
from its tribe to search a

      a bin and our pockets. It meanders carefree

           down the road and an MP names it 'Protection'

for a community under lupine siege, sturdy in
extreme unrest. Outside a church gate, in the absence of place and

company to enclose a feral heart, this wild beast
lets loose. A bullet wants to belong

        Bullet, strayed from the farm, seeks a home

          Bullet just wants to be loved.

Who will place a poster in a shop window asking *Have you
seen this bullet? Reward offered.*

      Watch how they deny owning that which

            foams viciously at the mouth.

WHEN YOU DID NOT WANT TO SEE BUT YOU CANNOT UNSEE IT

what can you do, but recall. A bell cannot unring a song that cannot be unsung
by petrol xylophones and baritone bricks who harmonise with a gravel choir
and a clave that executes four loud cracks: Accidentals? There is a reason there is
no such thing as a 4/3 time signature. It does not sound right to

our ears, in the same way the liquid crescendo will not seem right to the eyes.
A conductor can control his first violinist with a baton, or his eye
will announce the first beat in a bar, to a rapt audience waiting beside
our bored concertmaster who plays the same starting note for the thousandth time.

It is frustrating to have a tune stuck in your head, when you do not
know its name. Let us train our ears so we might know the melody
performed by thirteen wilting flowers and candles before the creaking double
whole note of a garden gate. Let us conduct ourselves accordingly.

I

From the midsummer height of Càireasbhal,

looking west over causewayed Dùn na Cille,

the sun has lit the townlands in the Gulf Stream's evening zephyr.

In the pellucid ocean light, under the troposphere's

argentine blue, everything comes into HD focus:

the blackland's dikes and rickety fences,

rush-fledged forage of tussock and rock,

fleece-shedding sheep and rough, red-pelted shorthorns;

Boisdale's straggle of crofts and cottages,

Nissen huts, tractors, jacked-up transits;

and the tracks beyond through the plain of barley,

to the sugar-sand crescent of Orasaigh Bagh.

Orasaigh, the double-humped tidal island

on the beach off the edge of the Boisdale machair,

still moored to her mother by the sand umbilicus

she fashions herself from the silts of the longshore drift.

She rises on her strand like a sagging frame tent,

Or the sunken withers of a sea-ware pony,

two shaggy rorquals, breaking the swell

from the Sound of Barra, frozen on the curve

towards Hirte and the Greenland seas.

The beach-stripping blitzkrieg of winter storms

and the rising tides of the gnawing Atlantic

have frayed, but not in centuries severed,

her squat tombolo's hawser. She will not let go

of the land that birthed her and to which she still belongs.

II

I walk the track from Leth Meadhanach
to the crossroads with the faded road
that runs from Pol a' Charra to the Ford.
A quarter-mile strip of rough and tumble grazing:
horsetails, juncus, clumps of yellow flag,
rocks breaching the turf like the hulks
of fossilised right whales. The isle lies flat
on the low horizon, crushed under the dome
of the huge Atlantic sky. Each crunching stride-length
lifts it taller, on the western skyline, the vistas
of my mind. I lift the loop on the five-bar gate
and pass between derelict lazybeds and a stand
of thin phragmites. Sheep scatter from the fences
at my bootscrapes. Greylags up their periscopes.
Redshank yammer from the trackside posts
and switchback lapwings puit and dive—a motorhome
rumbles down the track to the barbecue pits
and picnic tables of the Geàrraidh na Mònadh campsite.
Settling dust, crushed stone diminuendo:
corncrakes shorting from the eight-inch grass
under tremolo columns of larks;
ululating snipe traverse the argentinian blue.
The crossroads mark the blackland's end
and the start of a furlong of sandy machair,
the ever-unravelling remnant of the miles-wide
Bronze Age plain. I set a course across the headlands,
between rusty ploughs and abandoned rollers,
sunk axle-deep in the blown sand's sod.
The patchwork of barley and needlework fallow
lays down its quilt before me, washed green silks
with crimson crewellings, stitched with cobalt,
silver and gold—orchids and cornflowers,
birds-foot trefoil, daisies, clover, corn marigold.

The scuts of conies vanish down sand-chutes
and dunlin drag disingenuous broken wings.
Quail crawl through the bent like whistling field mice.
From halfway across the machair—between the abandoned
burial ground and the gutted net station—
the island rises from the swell like Surt.
I can feel the shush and thump of ocean,
breathe the beach's warm kelp breeze.
Patrolling herring gulls monitor my approach
and gannets plunge from the sky's high tower—
then the wind's in my face on the low dunes' ridge,
and there, beyond the precarious, hop-across causeway,
the storm-ripped ruin of An Doirlinn and the crab boats'
wedge of white van landing—twin-papped, raven-crested
Orasaigh stands on its strand before me.

and the night you saw it live

you screamed / catharsis
amongst the crowd / cried into
your five-quid can / of red stripe /

lipstick smudged / but who cares in the dark? /

And you danced.

I saw you dance /

god it is good to dance.

I thought you had forgotten

how to move.

When the allegations came out
you said nothing

but I know it's there.
I see the way you want to
dance."

//

"I was in the crowd

waiting for the support band

when a whisper ran through the room (like a river)

everyone went to piss / buy a pint / browse the merch /
check their phones /

(which is how
the rumour came)

I turned to the girl next to me
(she'd come from Sweden)

& her eyes wide (as apples) she said softly

(fuck)

//

but the night I saw it live

I peered hoarse through crowds of bodies in the same sticky space choking and crying as if they'd never been alive before and never would be again, which for all I know they never would be, and certainly my heart has never beaten since, and the lead singer held his hand out to us, and we yearned for it like disciples, like his touch could save us, like his words could absolve us:

I just wanted to talk about depression... because things aren't always easy, sometimes you struggle to get out of bed, I know, if things are hard for you right now... they're hard for me too... and it's not your fault, I just want you to know it's not your fault...

and how bittersweet the realisation that our faith was misspent, that just because we thought he recognised our sadness does not mean we were safe, but yes to answer your question, sometimes it comes on shuffle and before my brain has come online my body starts to move and grieve communal, my heart starts beating again, yes for a moment music does whatever it is that it does, which I surely cannot be blamed for, feminist morals aside, it happens beyond the brain, music, music, and so yes to answer your question my blood recognises it and my blood loves it and I think no matter what he did it always will, it is inside me the way we moved as a crowd, snake-like, seductive, screaming together
and I can see you disagree but I don't know what to say, I wish I had never heard it, but it's beyond my control, and that song is in me now, isn't it? and that's what happens when an album saves your life? if you cut me open it would still be there and that's no-one's fault, that's just what music does, isn't it? that's just love, just blood?

//

isn't it?"

//

There is a poem down there,

In the air castle of the barricades,

In the wreck of prose,

At the funeral of the muse,

In the folds of nonsense,

In the blasphemy, the nobility, and the rage

At the bedside of the rhyme.

The poem is a drum

At the whim of the madmen,

A dodo bird, a coin for the outcast.

The awareness in a moment of desolation!

It is wherever

      Reason is on its knees,

      Sufi is annihilated

      And all senses are active.

The poem is always a whizz

That does more work than noise.

Its glory is not in the acclaim,

But in its transient bloom

Breaking through,

      Once and for all,

The comprehension of the world!

For Aaron Kent

I break prose into poems
Like wood into a pyre.

Figures and symbols
Shape a mind
That gives birth
To presences, men and suns of images
Fashioned so precisely
That they arouse desire
Along the syllabic line of memory

Nothing remains
>   But deeds,
Shadows of a shade
Speaking a language
Of bullets and birds
Fell already
From the other side of the brain.

No one can equal
No one can hear
The sky is too high
>   For the dead
Wedged down the field.

September

BESTIARY IN WHICH I HAVE OFTEN BEEN WRONG

A few weeks later, I dream the bird is not dead. I dream it is alive and lives in a mall downtown. I dream it has grown large, the size of a turkey really, and has a long beak, like a puppet in a Jim Henson show, and has no feathers, is buzzed, and speaks to say it is living in a bucket. The mall is half-empty, a nest that has long been abandoned, and there is a corridor that opens onto the pavement on Chacon Street, where everything is covered in grease, as though the whole street is a giant parking lot where the same car each day leaks oil. I dream that I wake up and the moon sits like a broken button against the pale blue fabric of the air. And Buster, yet again, thinks there is another animal in the yard, is convinced there is an animal in the yard. There is nothing in the yard. And yet he runs from one ghost to the next. I dream this and think, as I imagine it, how sad it is to believe in something, how sad it is to be wrong. Or is it that belief is more real than what is real, that Buster is right, and the bird is really there? When it comes to Buster, I have often been wrong. I have often reprimanded him for barking at nothing, only to find an iguana shading under the old rusty galvanise in the yard, its claws like a falcon's talons.

DUNGENESS

It is seaword. It is salt. It is thrashing of arms and legs in
dusk and low tide. It is the tern plunging into a wave to find
itself and yet not finding itself. It is the six "visual scores" of the
poet, the seven lighthouses, that must be retracted, revised, re-written,
like the shoals beneath history. There is a desert in
California where only marigolds grow. It is the idea of a desert,
for the Met Office now says that, too, is a fiction. It is the world
contracted thus: into an endless ocean of shingle, endlessly thrown up.
It is the world's smallest railway, that playfully calls to us as we sit
in The Pilot eating fish and chips. It is the pair of shells I take back
with me to London, to Walthamstow, where a split leaf marks the
entrance to the marshes, where cattle once grazed, where Althea
McNish is on display in the William Morris Gallery and I can
recognise the quality of the tropical light dappling every single
shrub and flower on her fabrics and I think of the way the smaller
shell fits into the bigger shell like a couple spooning and I wonder
if you will keep this memento. You had always wanted to visit Prospect
Cottage, you say, cupping the shell in your hand as though this
is where it was meant to be. It is the unruly sun, that fades the
writing on the cottage wall. It is the boiling water from the
nuclear plant, which, through subterranean currents, nourishes the
sea and brings the birds. It is the wave after each wave of realisation.
It is the thought. It is the hope: it is not too late. It is too late for us.

THE RIVER OF DOUBT

The photograph was taken by the President's son. Kermit, as a child, was sickly but had a flair for language and reading. As a freshman, he accompanied his father on a year-long expedition in Africa. For another expedition, to South America, he delayed his marriage. Like his father, he contracted malaria on the trip. But evidence suggests he downplayed his illness to save medicine for his father's use. There is a picture of Kermit in the Amazon with a beard and a hat, his eyes knowing and silent, but mainly silent. There is a picture too, from years earlier, of him holding his dog Jack, who looks at some force in the distance, as the ochre light of late afternoon cries on the scene. Although partridges steal one another's eggs, Leonardo Da Vinci, wrote, the young, when they have been hatched, always return to their true parents. When Kermit died in Alaska he never knew if he pleased his father.

BIOPSY

I know you dread
words of confirmation.
I know you didn't sleep,
paced the house, disturbed the dogs,
confused them into thinking
time was altered:
how I wish.

The hospital again,
heart-sink smell
of disinfectant,
fluctuating tedium
of a waiting room,
the nurse's roll-call,
the daily list.

You, in my blue and white kimono,
slippers taken
from a holiday hotel,
nurse-led, disappearing
down a corridor;
breathe,
I've got your back.

Time passes quietly
a soap-blown bubble:
you reappear, stretchered
through double doors,

waving.
I breathe,
hello my love,
you're back.

HUSBANDRY

I'm pruning roses, cutting out dead wood.
Stop! commands the sun, *sit and look!*
she grabs me by the hand, makes me rest – true,
the gin and tonic helps, but mostly it's her warmth.

I pay attention to what attention brings:
hear the pregnant ewes close-cropping turf,
watch the dog's nose twitch, some rich language
like the bee's dance, unknown to me.
I smell engine oil and new-mown grass,
sink into the blowsy bosom of the heat.

I see you cross the garden, spade in hand,
I call out *two gin and tonics and I'm anyone's,*
wait – because of course you come, hold me, laugh,
as we discuss where to plant the roses for next year.

DYING FOR AUTUMN

You worry at the death
of small winged things
dying for autumn

the dragonfly, green iridescence
on a flower stem,
blue eyes burning

wings alive with tracery
her shrunken abdomen
with no more eggs to give

the dark red admiral, flutter-slow
and wavering, seeking hibernation
before the weather turns

the greenfinch espaliered
against a window
flying as the sun is low.

You rescue them, of course you do,
take them gently on your finger,
watch them cling

as if their lives depend on you.
Perhaps they do.
I hardly like to tell you of the bird

the dog laid at my feet today
mouth-gentled and feather-damp,
red-legged, eyes glassy

caught before her time was due.
I rescue her, of course I do,
set her free for you.

LANDSCAPE WITH NO HAT

I leave the house without an umbrella
and notice that it's raining. I grab a pigeon
and start wearing it as a hat. A man sheltered
under the shop's eaves compliments my look.
Let's paint a picture of your hat – he says
and we do. But in the painting, there is no hat or pigeon,
only a nude woman giving birth to the moon.

MOON LANDING

Where is my lover?
My lover is inside a conch shell.

Who is my lover?
My lover is Buddha's tiny umbrella.

What is the function of a tiny umbrella?
Little girls use it to protect them from ghosts.

Where do ghosts come from?
Ghosts come from duck eggs.

What is an egg?
An egg is the double of the moon.

Can bad girls like me reach the moon?
Yes, they can. With their pinky toes.
If their eyes are firmly closed.

POEM EXCLUDING SPRING
after Noah Falck

I wash your feet

until you become a cathedral.

At night I dream of daffodils

and recall that June is the luckiest month

to marry. I try to remember whose poem

it is that juxtaposes a winter strawberry

and a wedding dress.

I am beautiful, but lonely.

Many times, I wake up and find myself

at our wedding, dancing. The mother of the bride

is not my mother.

HAPTIC, COVID, PHILOSOPHY

Working on a new book, the production of this book, this new
book, the haptic presentation of the world when I am alone with
my speech, my thinking, when the business drops away. I rely on
visual fedback, sighted and sited. I rely on sound in this
instance to indicate the key has reached its destination - using
a mechanical keyboard. Quietude. Perhaps too alone with my
thoughts. I take senses for granted which is obviously a
misrecognition, a misunderstanding of the world and its
modalilities. I leave the mistakes present, I can't read back
what I'm writing, can't return to it, a form of rmemory
residence. To beetter co mprehen d the structures of thought.
Now I think I will return to the _reading_ of this; I sense too
many eorrors, incomprehensions... Reading now:

Working through the book introduction of the book
Which is largely written by typing with closed eyes, some small
dictation as well, during covid and post-covid, extraordinary
depression, too much wartime right-wing time, too much "on our
plate" so to speak, so to think and type, eyes closed, this is
the introduction. So about epistemology which it's based on the
haptic, touching the world through the pressure and knowledge of
the keyus - in fact I make less immeidate mistakes in this
format than when writing with eyes open - which is morethan a
curiosity, but something deep emerges about the nature of speech
and its relation to movement as well as sighting/citing/siteing
the world, so to type. There are compenations in philosophy for
touching what one writes "about" - becoming what one writes
"with" - a distinction which melds, melts, blends. So that. Then
at times dictating, also with eyes closed, as if speech,
Wittgenstein you do thatand it carries, carries itself, hurtles
itself, listener formations, as if there -)there_ is where the
philsophical lies (in both senses, all senses) of the word.

————

Elevator Music, or: Music Composed by the Elevator

W/ my eyes closed, I can still hear it. The storm was
tremendous, some flooding, things like that. We live on the
fourth floor. There are fi9ve floors. We take the elevator up
and we take the elevator down. All is smooth on our travels. The
storm was raging. The elevator shaft was leaking, oh! The
dripping in the shaft hit the top of the elevator cage. Must I
insist on telling you that this was all metal, all thin
somewhat, all resonant? On the way up and the way down,
dripping. On the way up, the frequencies were compressed; on the
way down, they were expanded. The rhythm and tonalities changed.
You must! listen to this all the way through, the rhythm picking
up towards the end. The elevator was both the instrument and the
composer. We just pressed the buttons. I believe this is
everywhere in the world but we must, absolutely must, become
attuned to hear it. The pulse, commbination of pulses,
frequences dissonant and consonant, the murmur and to be sure
the murmur from the very begining, water sloshing around

stromatolites, who knows what storms, trilobites scrouing the
bottom. But the elevator, the elevator! To be given this gift of
tuning into the murmur from the very very very least expeted
sources, surrounding us, knowing as we do, that these will
continue here, there, everywhere, after we are gone, after we
are long gone, after we are longer gone, and the longest of
which illimitless, after and perhaps elsewhere, our consiousness
bound too intricately to the ephemera of our brains, migraining
the graine, harvesting the mgraine, what stories what emissions,
what effusions, diminutions, expansions. The universe, the
cosmos, the multiverse, in the sound of an elevator! The
elevator! And on the fourth floor after the fifth floor and the
subground floor, we left, departing the music which continues,
in the space of silence where we were then (and now), and thus -

___

Can't talk in the pool

Eyes closed, the pool, trying to focus, think I have long covid,
not sure, the symptoms are there, all of them, in messy
(dis)order, the constant sudden descent into absolute
exhaustion, which is the meain , that's main one, mean as well,
following me everywhere, distending my thoughts, contravening
whatever it is I might be thiniing, the words rise like scum to
the surface, mistakes and all, the swill, somewhere I wrote
about sweill before, not sure: swill wills however, that's
definite, the hum of the dehumidifier covering up any other
thoughts that might be rising to the surface, actually the
humidifer, not the de- and I wonder why that came first to mind,
te heat's coming on now "to be sure" and I can hear it, that
rush of air, earlier mice in the heating system, various sounds,
there's a nation here which can be comforting. I stop for a
moment. The thoughts, NOT THE WORDS, come forth, in other
words, OTHER WORDS, it's that process I've been following, the
intermixture but having nothing to do with writing or reading,
nothing like that, it's all in the f9inger's ordinary dance by
themselves, errors and all. I let that _sink in_ as best I can,
When my fingers extend to the "farthest reaches" of the
keyboard, there I have a thought again: the shoreline, barrier,
corrisng-point to the normative of typing/language, being
living, surviving. I think with long covid perhaps I won't
survie that long and perhaps Idon't have long covid at all,
self-diagnosis always a trap.. From what I've read it's always a
trap, but the symptoms are there and in any case something's
radically wrong with my body, or so I think. The doctor will get
back to me eventually. It's been four months since covid
presented itself. It's long after the epidemic per se and I
never thought I'd get it,or it would get me. I stup, confused
for an instant, the flow is broken, there are errors, I'm not
sure where, something in my mind, subetrrraen ean, is dictating
this now, errror after error, there's no escape, I'm
heart-broken, distraught, there's no way out of this, the
horizon seems darker, forboding, perhaps I'm dreaming all of
this, the sound of the keys notwithstanding.

___

Presence, re-scents, pre-sense, pre-sents

Now this is interesting, my face feels as if it's on fire, I
have no idea why. But there's something odd; when I type with my
eyes wide open, I make more errors; the feedback loop is sent
through the visual, not only the haptic and thought, thinking of
the content of the writing, but derailed by the visible (no
wonder people meditate with eyes closed~~~~) - so perhaps this
prcoeeds more smoothly. The platform expands, the margines are
automatic, I needn't take care, in fact care, Sorge, is of a
different sort, the differential of the visible (so to say),
which seems also to bring ennui into play, an odd sadness or
visible (not sonic) coloration of the world, those gray days
when you think that perhaps grey/gray is a color/colour after
all. We treead constantly on the unknown, no, within the
unknown, no,permeated by absence, disarticulation or
articulation unrecognized as such. I stop and scratch my
shoulder, then return, recognizing the fluctuations of the body
at work here. I don't worry about spelling, placement,
unworrying, thought emerging, liquidity. In the distance, water
running in fact. The haptic/sonic sphere appears already always
expanding and expansive, -- just hearing singing in the
distance, it's stopped, the clatteering of the keys now 1-
something granular. It's hard to think complexity without
recourse to what has been written before, I ride the wave, the
crest, in a sense, of thinking, hoping my hands, the rest of me,
is/are properly positined. You get the idea, not Idea, but flux
which is continuous and emerging, coming forward, however
defined when nothing is seen as such and words all sound the
same with the clack of the keyboard, no harbingers of
emergence... all the content I need always aready present, or
rather, one, I, am in the presence of presence...

Thus

—

No deception in the night (for Karl Kraus)

So, there's something you want to write?
Yes, why my eyes deceive me.
How so, or in that it is...
Easier to write blindfolded, without distraction, than it is
when wide awake, eyes wide open, who know what that will bring.
And so? And so I continue in this fashion opening up to
language, ignoring font, case, barrier, margines, paragraph and
indentations; letus not worry about that at all, let us set that
aside.
Well and good, and then you have nothing more to say?
Except that language is or may be its own realm, its own
nation, living uder its own laws or lawlessness, a kind of
wilderness, Joshua trees for example, as long as there are no
fires.

TIGER WOMAN

it was dark giving birth in the belly of the whale

    no moon   no stars

just so many ribs and their ivory glow

All night the spirit tiger

prowls   strange in a flesh and water world

raises her heavy paws

steps across the father

asleep in the flood of the floor

you looked at me with dangerous eyes

through an armour of lashes you wore till the end

a small savage creature

holding your pulsing pushing egg

in pale thin arms

strapped and trapped

desperate to reach the mouth of the whale

push through the silver baleen

swim out and up

into the sparkling night

SEA WOMEN

my body stands like that
more liquid than a man's
I claim the mineral rights inherent in
my supplicating palms   this body mine
but mined and mined and never mine
the copper in the knee that pins the wind
iron smelted to steel within my mind
and I have cavities inside where I
have always been afraid
man spins his wool of words   he clothes us
now we swim   naked in the white wash
striking out   for somewhere new
where we have never been
and never been and never been

MEDICINE

earth-body alchemist

finger and thumb

pinching the shaft of an owl's feather

dancing the sea-spiral

dressed in darkness

dense as the derelict mines

under our hills

weaving energy

into that vital stone

arms   scything serpents

legs beat the mud drum

follow the sand song

I sing through my bones

you who turn oil into flight

fear my prayer

hear it coming like weather

warm front

storm dark

a spinning canticle

pulling it

all to ground

October

*

Noriaki stille
som en knokkel
over kulen

Noriaki quiet
as the white knuckle
of the hill

*

regn over Sanru-elva
Noriaki fisker
kirsebærørret

rain over the Sanru River
Noriaki fly-fishes
cherry trout

*

hoppbakken i
Shimokawa, dufter av
Noriakis barndom

the flying hill in
Shimokawa, hints of
Noriaki's childhood

*

*

raus Noriaki
signerer ansiktet
til månen

generous Noriaki
signs the face
of the moon

*

himmelen spenner
buen, Noriaki
blir en pil

the sky opens
the bow, Noriaki
the arrow

*

i sommerhuset
under en vinterfrakk
Noriaki sovende

in a summer house
under a winter coat
Noriaki sleeps

*

*

Noriaki
en fugleunge
før sitt første hopp

Noriaki
a baby bird
before his first leap

*

mens vi venter på
Noriaki, hopper
Godot bakken ned

while we wait for
Noriaki, having gone
Godot is ground down

*

i Engelbergluft
som mørkner
flyr Noriaki

in Engelberg air
darkening
flying Noriaki

*

BLUE (1993)

A pool, the sky, a wrapper flapping in the wind, a woolen scarf, a rhinestone
mobile, stained glass mottled on a moonlit road, the stripe on a stray beach ball,
a lost song, a last psalm, an adulterous husband and wordless daughter, below
the belly of a speeding Saab the asphalt is muted beryl, rain in a sky outside blue
walls, a man in a sodden blue shirt escapes a suddenly empty house, *liberté, égalité,*
fraternité across a parking lot, swimming laps by herself, cutting through the
bucolic grounds, crossing littered arrondissements, a lady game to jaywalk who is
hypnotized by headlights, white coat reflected in a close-up of her pupil, bottomless
against a bloodshot white, hands flipping a lighter as a neighbor timidly knocks, a
face reflected from a bare shoulder, a ring that glints under naked bulbs, a crucifix
on a clerical smock, 'I want no possessions, no memories, no friends, no lovers—
they're all traps'.

PRIX FIXE, LUNDI

Listen, I just couldn't text you back. I was rifling through a bin of panties in Paris. 'Voila!' a diligent brunette said. 'C'est bonne!' declared a blonde. I stashed a blue green number in a metal basket. I bought silly man-undies of which I'm sure you would approve. I don't mind the cigarettes, if the ceiling feels heavenly. I fully intend at eighty to smoke after any and every glass of wine. It occurs to me now that you are that glass, that pretzels taste better than they ought to. When the sun comes out, two women in hats approach with fruit in a wooden bowl. Starved lips in the gloom, you select two cherries.

WHITE (1994)

A frayed tag, a collar hugging a staid tie, the breast of a pigeon on courthouse steps, a boxy hatchback, metro tile, dirty snow outside a train, a toilet lid lifted to welcome vomit, smug at the stand with Veronica Lake hair, the echo of bridal heels down the aisle as she greets the white sky and white rice in a white veil, magnificent teeth in a giant smile, shivering on the street, a corduroyed crotch kneaded by a white palm, smuggled back home in an oversized bag, a rococo statue of a milk maid in the window, a portrait of the virgin and child in a rural Polish cabin, staging a funeral with a stranger's corpse, climax after 24 seconds of missionary bliss, through opera glasses, a prison cell. 'If I say I love you, you don't understand. If I say I hate you, you don't understand'.

*

Amongst them I found behind whenever you remember: prepare a meal for God. A lighter touch, toy soldiers rescale. This edge, again, of how far to dress up, curate and present the desperate and contingent. Realised I'd interpreted space behind as moving backwards.

*

Held at home, air is dance; both truth. How to do it for range, permission, decision? I make it will align not by knowing. At the shed, takes time to distinguish at this stage. Open we fall back. Decision is not levels of safety. No need to dream.

*

Does not get disturbed, doesn't tolerate. Give up some control. Not exactly not knowing. Transition between phrases – content of move. Learn to want more – if the ideal to stay in that space could I take it? Virtual head work, fear has manifested inside the rhythm.

*

Continuation of contempt – various contemporary factions, a less encumbered state. Again today feeling. Daily lines just now, a better foil. The table, the sign, the silent scream. Holes in the space of the words. Awareness and naming of disgust – at least two generations of blocked artists adapt to the idea of the dream.

*

Thinking of reading an idea, a trigger in the body means up. Holding breath, core muscles, works for us. Trying to connect to everyday movement – the invitation to expand passes through us. How to use last night's trigger? Have I rejected it for so long I can't change?

*

How to start to unravel? Cut out from forms into goals: celebrate, complain, commemorate. Slip in a varied formal history to suggest options. Neutral tense hopeful, polarity of body and form. The point of the form of the body is to move. We can't reach partners now.

*

Present inside the moving unfolding: oblivious, aware, hiding. Can't see who's looking. Fall into space as if surrounded by it entirely, move as it. Where is your pleasure? Vulnerable in our headlong progression. Moving with and into: take it in turns to suffer.

*

for Sarah Oktay

Softening to receive the space in front: quiet steady flame tending pliant. What have you missed? What do you not see? Comparing a key principle, same game: cross the threshold. Risk shame, transducing spiral of sound, echolocation. Tether yourself, turn the page: taken by eminent domain.

*

i.m. Louise Woodcock

In the blue hour: thread inside the available giving being received. Impress, surrender to impulses which do not contradict. In the blue hour, what is it other than to live, drop to integrate? Technique to instigate courage to sink deeply into the real. The blue hour: where does it initiate? Let go of naming.

*

Love and its inevitable plurality: when memory spits in the face of power. Lapwings, sorrel, lady's bedstraw beside the reservoir. It feels like I've done everything right to be here today. Large reverse strides with alternating legs, transferring weight, changing direction. The grass lit by the lantern in the park – as if tenderly enfolding the night – how to be a good friend? How to remember what you love, how to love, how to remember? In our reduced state, mist rising in the field at midnight.

*

Sustained radical simplicity, continuous present, combat burnout. Slow, weighted mind of organs, counter-cultural. What are you touching? Make sense by moving and leaving traces, take responsibility for your physical self.

MORNING SONG
After Sylvia Plath

My own cry was just as bald, primal
lunging at the elements undomesticated
animal, language of blood-ripe-banana-peel

I slipped along sanitised air and effaced
my parents in stretches of screams, tore
at the small hours and howled out

for morning to burst at my seams–
the gold watch of sun was swallowed or
I think it swallowed me, ingesting my name

who in my stomach sits cow-heavy, cringe-stained
a pregnant cloud refusing its rain, I spat light
until our room is haunted and spinning and

maimed. Some world to rise just like balloons:
rubber, bitter, too much too soon.

BECOMING ECO-FRIENDLY

Became something like a three figure income, tasted
like avocado and chia seeds, felt like

Patagonia.

Became breadline scapegoats: no Primark,
no meat no cling film, became

a shopping isle filled with protein balls
and other vegan delicacies, became

no ham sandwich for school so I
stopped eating.

I could be more grateful for middle-class friends.

For sleepovers at the second-house, Clare's
pesto passed around between freelancing. I offered
up the silence–tongue biting–not hearing

her screwed up eyes on my cheap chav shoe
still, I spun fuck yous into thank yous
never questioned the holidays abroad,
the string of amazon parcels or
her cupboard of food miles, hid
my curiosity on the number of lights
strung above each fireplace.

One time though, Clare asked me
to take one of her shiny metal bottles
from her bright kitchen island.
I said I reuse my plastic Evian one
just fine. She said she wanted to help me
be more eco-friendly. I said thank you.

CHEAT DAY

Caught on my tongue, I want
to swallow this crime whole.

Normally, our eyes don't meet
along the isle, you're on the side

I abandoned so you could trust
me, you still

trust me at the checkout, on
the counter, by the sink you

hoped I meant to bless back
breath from boiling water.

I hate to think the last life
you heard was potatoes

peeling, fat frying

me– I want to say it was worth
something but you–

tasted like betrayal. What a shame
to know, in all your impending doom,

I still broke our promise
of protecting you.

CORONA TO 'CORONA'

Once you had autumn in your palm.
You made a garland of the coronach, twisted
the lovers' twig arms
and falcate leaves into coronation.
The lovers called to God bare-faced, *It's time*
you saw us, God, us lovers,
standing here corona to corona.

Now in the wreathing of years
the word breathes differently —
a virus old as love and new as every
lover's new mutation.

ICE, EDEN
after 'Eis, Eden'

There is a land called Lost, a moon
is flowing in its reeds
and everything once frozen
as we were frozen sees

and warms its power of vision
from two bright earths. The night,
the night, the lye's corrosion
this eye-child brings to light

It sees it sees we're seeing
thou seest and I see
this time of ice, its freeing
from time, its rising free.

PTSD: THE POET'S NIGHTMARE

Moonless raining crystal hurled from the shop
stumbled dash through fire-fall up and into
the hissing house-sized truck
pulled in, parked up, parked right here on the mind-scene's
cries unseen made scene of...
  Cut out the punning, can't you?
    ... mad scene un-ensouling. Blood is glass. My feet keep slipping.
Overcoats sprawled old men bat-naked. *Please calm down.*

Poem and Poet wrestle pointlessly.
Poem sweats, pleads,
Stand still a moment, will you.
Let's prise you free of me.
Time to let go. Ouch, let's go! Move it, b-b-
bastard, or else be handed over
to Commentary Cathedral.
Poet shrinks, jumps into Poem's string-bag.
Poem sighs, somehow shoulders the weight.
If he can't take me
today he can't not take me. I'm his transport.

November

SUNLIGHT

no longer hesitant in the widening gaps
no longer lost

where spider mites made their thin kingdom
till the tower of it

settled for brown. Little skulls
for flowers by the end. The birds it wore

haven't so much flown
as melted, liquid

quickly. Every sawn
and pointing limb coming plucked

like a feather, replaced
by this fingerless breeze. Staring through

we grow younger, we grew
with this sentinel. These careful, steady cuts

carve the old tree back
to light, more light and nothingness

WHAT WERE YOU, SPIDER

if not the unflushed hauled back up
on luck and your knee-knuckles? Not much more
than the bones of a tent
with its top whipped off. Breeze-

dried through, you retuned
as the many-armed harpist, all prongs for strings
to pluck to shivers, to strum
in sun for a day. At first you lived giddily

on a windowsill, then on tenterhooks
on a thinning crochet clinging to its pin, catching
airborne banquets, falling
horizontally. Rain came

lending globes for your orrery, but the cold
made your domain craze
like a trodden mosaic, overcrowded now
with no guests and no busy maker

except what's left in the neatening frost
in which you've formed, like grief, this brittle stylus
of yourself, this crisp claw
to needle an infinite spiral.

HONOURING THE ANCIENT DEAD

No matter what you see of age
or illness, disaster, ritual, or war, remember

while you learn, no fragments found
behind this glass

could be my love, nor all my knowledge
nor all yours.

You may not chance to share
this air, although you might reflect

the heart and vision that you are
is also how I was. Release for me at least

a breath, a tiny, living wish for peace. Then breathe
as if for all of us.

SAY WHAT YOU LIKE

about Hendrix playing alone in his bedroom
it can sound a lot like vertigo

say what you like about a nervous breakdown
it can look a lot like summer

all the chords slip off the guitars and pool
on the floor like cuts from the rushes

Orpheus meanwhile is drinking in the Underworld
nothing like a tall cold Lethe and grenadine

on a day like today when all you can hear is the heat
nonetheless some feelings are like

radioactive spiders you can't kill them
however hard you try and it seems

important to people that I eat more chlorophyll
but I am full to brimming on the buttery

electricity that animates this extraordinary
corpse of mine this magnificent scaffold

and the spirit of my mother drops
into the room like honey into tea and I ask her

what she thinks about all this and she makes known
(she doesn't speak exactly) that this sunshine

and sweetness are all that's left, actually,
when you get to where she is so I say the sooner

we get there the better right and she doesn't laugh
exactly but I remember how alike we are

she too liked to live life as an arrow
in flight and was careless with her aim

very well then set the metronome to half
a heartbeat per minute and let's dance

to the rhythm of the song of whales slower
than the roots of trees and the orbit of Neptune

EPITHALAMION
for Tom McLaughlin and Fernando Cabral

The doves of Brazil may be reckoned thus:
the quail doves — sapphire, ruddy, and violaceous;
the white-tipped dove; gray-fronted and eared doves;
and the ground doves — blue and blue-eyed, scaled
and ruddy; common and longtailed; plain-breasted;
purple-winged; and picui. The doves of Ireland
are fewer. They comprise the rock dove and
the stock; the mourning; the European turtle;
and the collared dove native to Eurasia. Aphrodite's
bird is modest. Gentle colours suit her best:
creams and greys, sometimes a dappled prism
at the neck that gestures to the glory of emerald.
Such a soft and muted thing is love, a double-hearted
being that nestles and conjoins in a symmetry of feeling.
Both your breaths animate the throat of a flute
in a woodwind chorus: two lovers lay aside the things
of courtship, the striving and the coy, and beak in beak
grasp hold and bow, each to the other. The scene
plays out on every street. Hail Hymen, king
of wedlock! Ajoiner, bringtogether, encompasser!
In his name, I wish you pigeon blessings.
Bend, always, to love. Dovelike ever recall him,
that magnetic miracle, your personal north.

Coda

Imitari, resemblance of memory. I have been portrayed,
represented, as if this were the fair copy of a life.

The first thing I remember, I was sitting on the toilet,
and fell in, convinced I was to be flushed down the dark

mouth of the drain. I remember a hot pulse of lightning
thrashed inside my body, before the rescuing of hands.

But no, this is not the first thing I remember. There was
a sound first, or the scattering of a sound, like an image

trapped in a kaleidoscope before shaken loose. Sometimes
I hold it up to the sky and the glass around my brother

                                                breaks.

AFTER A TORRENT

In your sackcloth loin robe, look up—
a raven's beak is delivering bread
above your head, as in Preti's St Paul.
Look up—hang your coat from a hook
on the wind's back, tilt your breath
to the sky and dream, primordially,
as if you knew how to fly through
pitchfork rain. Clouds pass inside
your blood quicker than the turning
of a key. Childhood spins: a carousel
rusted out among beech leaves.
You live on, morphologically, as if
by afterthought, wondering why time
is rarely dignified by acts of time-
less charity. Sunset's purple garter
breaks on yellow satin. Touch of hands
above a petroleum-skinned city.
Santiago, Paris, as you wish it—
every mix of colour defines the self
transfigured, every form imitational
essence. Brancusi's primal cry echoes
the tearing of light. Inhale to exhale.
Look up—a rabbit moon silhouettes
the coastal road over Celastun,
irradiating sorrow, condolence.
You live with all the unsayables
in your voice when saying goodbye.
You take the bread in your mouth,
and carry on with somewhere to get to.

NEMINIS

He said his wife gave birth to their inner child.

He said the world's water flows through a single tap.

He said Mercutio was a hothead in a quadrangle.

He said only fishermen sing the river's soliloquies.

He said he lives and dies by The Nether Lodge.

He said moonlight is the most imitated form of nature.

He said even the clouds are known for putting it on.

He said: who do you think you are, one of the three Brexiteers?

He said rainbones clattered in his father's voice.

He said his mother was from a rare breed of three-headed sabres.

He said the grandest lunacy is yet to come.

He said professionalism is the rife of doom.

He said Cyclops calls the sheep in from the fell.

He said Dryope speaks to him on the heath in mirror code.

He said Mountbatten believed in angel aviaries.

He said the wheat fields are cotted with blood.

He said he spoke loudest in bed.

He said the car waiting outside is the coffin.

He said it takes a shovel to dig the southern palace.

He said the worst kind of talk is blowpipe.

He said the best kind of nightmares are calligraphic.

He said blue is the most echoic colour.

He said television is the longest-running cartoon.

He said Trident is sharpening for Poseidon.

He said Galileo never took their word for it.

He said he always reads the parentheses first.

He said the Vatican got drunk on Maron's wine.

He said they believe in the official version of difference.

He said the wasp stores its last sting in the villages.

He said he was made to feel like a pigeon statue in an empty square.

He said all power is malarial.

He said foliage is really submarine.

He said to look out for the shadow curtain.

He said his name was Neminis, nobody among men.

IN OTHER EYES, THE ARCHIVE HAPPENS

In his image, all is created. This is the arch-creator worshipping his image by seeing it as the only rightful heir of the face. In the photograph before us, creation is carved from within, meticulously molded into multiplicity: the man photographs the child and the photographer photographs both the photographer and the photographed to archive photography, alongside the preceding eyes, as distinct times. Before I enter the photograph, I wait on the edge, to borrow some time from this endlessness. There are disparate footprints, traces of the man and the child, and of those who preceded them or have just passed. The camera, inside the photograph, is pointing slightly downwards to match the child's height and capture his small stature as he treads along. It is a jovial view and yet appears to quickly transition into a dead end even though they are still somewhere in the middle. It is a photograph-narrative, a throbbing memory, coupled with the sudden realisation that those inside will unknowingly venture into the outside world, thinking that living, in this instance, outside the photograph, always happens in the aftermath of a photograph.

THERE WILL ALWAYS BE A VENDOR BEFORE AND AFTER THE PICTURE

It is a photograph of a coffee vendor in motion; of somebody who is familiar enough with the routes of the camp to roam them with relative ease.

The clanking of the cups, emanating from the collision of two porcelain cups – fragile but not too fragile – in the vendor's hand, can still be heard or seen from beyond the picture.

But what is the clanking for? What does it signify amongst other signifiers, in a noisy context such as the camp where sounds continually fight for a space to be(come) sounds.

The truly inaudible clanking is nothing but a testimony of arrival into a place, a shibboleth, a different dialect.

The vendor will soon escape the picture or be pushed away by another.

However, somewhere, there will always be a vendor before or after the picture, or more precisely inside of it, boiling his coffee in silence.

EXISTING IN ANTICIPATION

Details are for those in a hurry not the seer. Seeing engenders its own details – details that seem to happen in the folds of the seen with minimal reverting to what comes before and after the photograph. The photograph moves towards light, from a tunnel-like state to a quasi-resolution that is cut short by the wall of a house at the far end. This is the rite of passage, ours, to corners concerned above all else with the very meaning of living as a pact with memory. The hanging cables act as an arbour of some sort, a material shading in the absence of a sky that is lost on its way to the camp while the ground offers a path that appears well-trodden and distant at the same time. Bins, green in colour, placed on each side of the alley with differing visibility, echoing the green door towards which the woman in black slowly moves, all preceded by a mound of rubble and disparate and barely visible doorsteps. As we glimpse the woman in motion, balancing a shopping bag in each hand, veiled and draped in an abaya, the physical end of the photograph gradually intersects with the beginning of the woman's anticipated disappearance. Three figures to her left, one poking out, two standing, one holding a brown plastic chair as though gesturing towards the end of a time spent outside or the initiation of a new one. While this is part of an alley in Baddawi camp, it emulates other places where entering and exiting a place is on a par with sparing a moment to count your limbs, to check they are still with you. The woman could be my sister. Or a neighbour growing into distance to approximate her shadow. This is definitely walking in the footsteps of a time that is far away.

I wake each day with my morning hair full of takeaway grease / My head sliding from the quiet happiness found in dreams where I'm confident in a floral shirt / or the concentrated energy of nightmares where I lose my genitals / I feel most at ease in a state of consciousness where I watch the action of others / or myself moving in and out of erratic rusted chainsaw motion / In these conscious states my name is pronounced with the same involuntary smile a mouth makes when it asks for strawberries / In those subconscious states I punch with the efficiency of a Catholic mass at a rave / but there is no violence until I'm attacked by a feral black dog / it rips at my larynx and my thighs / I feel nothing because I'm a spectator / I don't die because dying can't happen / I'm needed elsewhere / needed as a father / my greasy hair lumbering into participation always being poor and late for the bus / always stinking with cheap lager breath / washing up last night's arguments and my girlfriend hates me / where is the dog / he's late

The bruises on my thighs are all the flat keys on a piano
I'm looking for that break in the sequence that might
Arrive timetabled in a key change or with friends knocking on the door
I'm fearful of my forced relationship with brass belt buckles
Scared my accent will burn the roof of my mouth
Or having to learn outdated dad voices
Afraid my sperm won't work and my drama could never be serialised
Panicked my Adam's apple will rot from the base
Terrified I'll have my jaw cracked like a bad joke
Wild birds migrate out of the postcode of me
Pulling away from the polite posture of my winter hair
I think about fashioning an unexceptional pair of wings
It will be made from lost pubic hair and day-old takeaway chicken bones
Hopeful of joining the birds and no longer having to taste cigarette ash and petrol

The shadows which emanate from all the men I've known

Visibly made up of the frailty of poorly settled jelly

The futile fight of a single ice cube sat in grandad's whiskey

Tasting just the same as the weakness which comes from seeing

Your blood or vomit

For the first time

Each river surges with catholic guilt

There is a finite volume of water my legs can resist

Before being reduced to a water bead

Some men can't help but move with the swell

Feeling the current of each day's venom my the ribcage

The trees which bear fruit watch me in the stream

Offering a branch to pull me from the wake

A rotten disease beneath the surface allowing them to snap in my grasp

December

LIVES OF THE SAINTS

I
NUMBER ONE

Which might just be something specific to the afterimage
of an empirical society and I guess it's a question of
whether or not there's much value in worrying about
methodology or thinking about the question of social
organisation and no matter what we might want to say
about management or teleology they're both just
dependent on the question of cause and I had stupidly
thought that Arnold's book was going to be about the
variability of culture and how it exists previous to our
understanding of it or the way that culture is nothing
except a refactoring of the non-sensible into the sensible
but really he just seems to talk about reticence and
cause and I guess it's that 'I think that the artists who
aren't very good should become like everybody else
so that people would like things that aren't very good'
which is still just that the intelligibility of anything is
always just the intelligibility of some previous state of
affairs which is still really just only about an older belief
in a particular understanding of the movement of time
which to me is only just a bare and somewhat foolhardy
commitment to the lasting efficacy of cause.

II
OR THAT

it's the readability of the poetic line or more than any-
thing it's the lyrical proposition of the thing and no matter
my feelings toward you or the collective will of ours toward
history or the balkanisation of the state it's forgetting
which is the supposed progressive idea of language
being the bulwark of memory and trace or the recognition
of trace and the repetition in which it's the very idea of
trace that is underwritten in the perspectivist longevity
of trace and it's that repetition is itself just change in the

longue durée which as in the contextualisation of the thing
or the actual density of a line built up and the particular
coherence of gravity none of this being choice but only
our situation being previous to the invention of the ideal
or the repetition of form which in the opposition to a
monist realism there's nothing that we can say about
the line other than that it's just the return of the same
which laid out across the moment of the lyric is change.

III

all of which is just the question of whether or not we
can have some criteria against which the poem is able
to be judged or the idea that there is an outside to the
informational question of judgement or the communica-
bility of judgement and it's about the supposition of
certain sets of particular facts which is really just a
question of judicial selection or the bracketing off of
certain parameters toward the claim of phenomenolog-
ical experience and in that there's a need for the delineation
of certain understandings of horizon or the possibilities
of the repeatability of phenomena which are not such
as the specificity of texture or the absence of texture but
for some reason I always think that you're unhappy with
me or that I'm somehow screwing things up and it's that
I don't seem to have any real purpose with things and
maybe there are other methods of reparative behaviour
or things I could do differently but the difficulty is maybe
to be able to feel the quality of a work without any recourse
to empiricism or the supposed coherence of reason or as
to be able to measure the absence of an historical trace that
being the central problematic in the differentiation of cause.

IV

Which is explainable to what largely and it's intimidating
to think about the wholeness of a poem or the image of
a poem or at least academically and I wonder if you had

ever imagined New York differently all those years or at
least in the articulation of things as we think about them
to ourselves and it's the description of the poem to itself
or as accidentally to thyself of the egalitarian of the existing
and non-difference and 'one night I dreamed that I painted
a large American flag and the next morning I got up and I
went out and bought the materials to begin it and I did'
which as with realism is the impulse of difference and
maybe this is the logic of the poem which is difference or
the similarity of the image of the state to its memory instead.

V

and despite their own problems Western democracies
seem to be less capable of managing themselves
these days and maybe saying 'these days' is a bit
short-sited or is ignoring too much and it's like Clause-
witz or Foucault's reading of C. or like how information
systems are never a solution to material problems
or like the way that politics has been subsumed into a
more general physicality of intents and causes and I
mean is politics even a thing anymore like it was in
2006 or in the hangover of the post-Soviet years and
maybe it's not even a problem of democracy but it's
about the incapability of politics and the question of
how to manage anything other than just by the sheer
force of it and I guess I hope that there's some way
we can organise ourselves better in the future or I mean
is it even an epistemic question anymore or is it just
that there's no possibility for the management of change
and maybe we just shouldn't worry about things or
maybe it's really just that Hayek's theories about markets
and pricing signals were always just fucked up anyway.

AFTER WORDS

Tarmac gleams under rain, a strip
of polished iron, a blade
in which you might catch the glimpse
of an enemy face. Don't ask
for directions. It's better not to know.

Gracious the tall poplars which lean
so near to each other, along the road south.
'We have seen too much,' they whisper,
'we will give nothing away.'
Silent the long fields. Which have suffered most.

LOOKING FORWARD

That year the mornings wore the drab of asphalt
levelled over corpses, the skies of Europe
hung in deep folds as if they could drop snow
on you and you and you

yet also

in hidden valleys frost spun lace across
burgeoning trees.

SURREAL DISUNION

Although a special part of its function is to raise a flag of truce
on the roof, it examines with a critical eye
the phosphorescent door, impossible
to assign borrowed clothes to the negation
of an unrecognisable shape. The entire aim
is a fog to cut with a knife. The notion
that cynicism is not enough, our allegiance being
to dreamers at the point of departure
is no way to play on words. Most certainly
wrestlers benefit from training
in the possibility of a week of Tuesdays.
Under these circumstances the day of tears
is passed in playing up the contradictions
between the open palm and the cupped hand.
I do not believe the reason it is done
would invalidate a single word.
The loner at the feast has no intention
of granting elegance to the Freudian concept
of singing out of tune. Surrealism demands
you get into the envelope of the sky
without knowing how to swim.

THE BEAST AND THE GYRES

> *and all things run*
> *on that unfashionable gyre again.*
> — W. B. Yeats

An anthropomorphic about-turn, as gods climb free of icons,

      and you, you scowl,
      because *only* still a

      man on all fours; for

only as a portent in the goggling eye of some haruspex or priest
      can you be known.
      You, sat hunched at

the womb-door of Mary, unable still to comprehend good *or* evil,
until the next generation wheels back in Christ's mannequin,

      and epistemologists in
      the pope's head build

a mind-sized matchstick model of the universe...when

      God, *before* atheism,

he fails to kill off the human virus growing inside of him,

      allowing Hitler to be born
      (sin to suppurate science).

When all Homo sapiens feel it: your beast-tail at their coccyx,
a lion's paw instead of a hand; as Buddhists atop mountains

      abort their bodies,
      to breathe back *your*

      body into the void...

While World War II struggles now to reach a beach, and the
disembodied are impeached, as Nietzsche's soul returns,

when heaven-wasted muscle attaches once more to living bone,

     and in a new cone we
     hear a phone ring, as a

blackhole, it narrows into the horn of the first wax cylinder phonograph

to play *your* voice? to earplug the damned and/or force the saved
     to raise a mirror and *deflect*
     God's light away from them,

     to leave their attenuated

rapt trunks to blink alone in blackness... as you, the beast,
you squeeze into the passage at Thermopylae, where even

     worms start to mistake
     your spear holes for the

     five holy holes in Christ...

For like castrato singers with laryngitis, the angels in heaven
     now cannot sing, and
     all love for God it dies,

     until Dante is born and

those in the Empyrean drool, to watch collapse (again?) the gyre
     unable still to release you.

While you, anaesthetized by sin, you wait, with a hypothetical yet
     serrated grin, for all time?

until your own church, from behind the clouds emerges, and the whole
of Christianity is reduced to the unexploded hand grenade of your heart,

>pinless and ready now to
>blast Christ apart, if God

>imagines *you* on the cross...

On the day when Kierkegaard and Hegel in a corridor meet, and you,
>you wake up swaddled still
>in Yeats soul, like a thermal

>foil blanket draped about you,

to keep *you* alive long enough for thought to outthink thought... and for

>one final appearance of
>Caesarism to subjugate who?

As you, through the final rusted drainpipe of a gyre you drop,
>to *stop* history repeating

>itself with your birth.

WINDSCREENS

Some deer ran onto a train track, which soon became a descent to hell.

There should be no deer in hell, said someone watching through a crystal-ball-like device, but more modern and Scandinavian in design.

It seemed to be some kind of administrative error, which no one could undo.

So they sent in a swat team, rescued the deer and brought them back into the world.

But the deer weren't really deer afterwards, so affected were they by flashbacks and nightmares.

Woe betide anyone with heated seats who offered them a ride.

Many windscreens were shattered in the Syracuse area.

PHILOSOPHY

Some deer responded to a call.

With trepidation they made their way to the centre of the forest.

A woodland creature, a kind they had never seen before, was stuck in a wire.

It seemed to be ashamed of its pain, something the deer had not encountered before.

What was this shame, they asked each other, in deer language.

It appeared that this poor woodland creature had been spending too much time with humans and their toxic ways.

How very sad for it, the deer agreed in deer language, unaware that at some point during the discussion the creature had died.

COUNTRY

Some deer wanted to frolic, cavort and copulate 24/7.

This was all well and good, said one of the more sensible deer, but they had received a warning from the Nostradamus deer to say that if they did, something bad would happen.

The deer thought the soothsayer was scaremongering and continued to do exactly as they wished.

It was then that a country and western festival started in all deer populated areas.

Everyone knew how much deer had an aversion to country and western music and felt for them, truly, as their cavorting came to a sullen end.

THE ONLY UNBROKEN BENCH

The ice-cream van is gone for the night, and the children
with their pockets full of crusts and lettuce.
The ducks have buried their bills in their feathers.
At the doors to The Pike a light is blinking,
a coin in the gutter blinks up – a face
you don't have a name for. You drift
round the newsagents, its avenues of milk and biscuits,
bin bags and wine. You swing on the swing
where the argument happened, pass the chippy,
the chemist, the nail bar, the allotment, the gate
to your heart is in constant use, there's a lorry
parked across it. Why do you always find yourself here
when the girls are asleep in your childhood bed?
The river is sullen, one wooden rowing boat
drugged by a streetlight, not yielding to the current,
not struggling against it. Your parents watch Casualty
in separate rooms. You swam hard and fast and away.
Now you float, lungs filled with night-time,
back towards the flicker of two televisions.

THE NEIGHBOURS ARE ARGUING ABOUT THE STARS

whether it is, or isn't, Orion's Belt.
I'm lying in the total dark in the new house
with the Artex, the serving hatch,
the symmetrical windows we both loved.
A hand on my tummy scanning for a signal.
A hand on my breast pressing for tenderness,
pushing harder into sleep. It's happening again –

I rev its engine, but the day won't start.
I see your shadow on the landing, telling me
it's time now. You lounge on the counter,
I rinse the mugs, you chatter at the sparrows
nesting in our gutters, dipping to the borders,
calling to each other. Coffee on the sofa
with a space between us and you always fill it.
Tell me you're *not* a motor that runs on love.
My body is a taxi – it gets me to the office,
to Asda, to mum's house. I put cat food
in my trolley, pizza in my mouth. I laugh,
answer *hmm* or *no*. All we talk about is you –

your white belly fur, those tiny incisors,
the way you supervise the pigeons,
nose the sparrow yolk crusted on the patio.

STILL LIFE

There are thousands
of varieties of apple
to consider.

You stand like a vase
anxious to be filled
with an armful of roses.

The vanity mirror
unveils the answer –
unbearably, it's you.

Grapes slouch over grapes.
The point of the knife
addresses you directly.

A fly makes a fuss
about the mackerel
and it should.

You hover by the easel,
no colour on your brush
but you focus on the fly.

The orange becomes
an orange as you
pick it up and peel it.

PROSE

The night skies of my London childhood were drowned in streetlight and when I looked upwards, all I could ever see was the Moon with its features blurred by clouds and pollution. The planets and the stars were neither more nor less than pictures in books; I learnt the constellations from small black and white photos in one of Patrick Moore's guides to astronomy, the grain of the film still visible on the page. My children's encyclopædia had an entry for the Universe showing an expanding balloon covered with black dots for galaxies. I had no real idea what 'Universe' or 'galaxies' meant, but I was drawn to the words themselves. The encyclopædia also told me that the Sun was actually a star and furthermore it was a radio star, and I marvelled at this apparent connection with the metal box that bristled with buttons and dials, and sat on the kitchen counter, its antenna pointing up at the kitchen ceiling. What could the words 'radio' and 'star' possibly have in common? But I loved the phrase 'radio star', and would repeat it to myself, perhaps because it hinted at another sort of reality, a different type of truth encoded in the words. For me, 'radio star' was a poem.

When I left London at the age of eighteen and moved to Leeds to study physics and astronomy, I realised that cities did not stretch endlessly to the horizon and that the night sky was not tinted orange. Here, I was taught how to look properly at this sky, to train my eyes to become dark-adapted by turning away from the surrounding buildings and car headlamps, and patiently waiting before I could make out dim stars, the merest twinkles of light.

This mini apprenticeship I underwent each cloudless evening gave me a chance to appreciate the stellar landscape. I learnt to navigate around the sky from the ladle of the Plough to the Pole star. This new-found ability revealed for me not only well-known constellations such as Orion or Cassiopeia, but also the smaller, fainter targets of my academic enquiry. Ever since, I have associated the Hyades stellar cluster with standing on the roof of Leeds University's physics department, and getting a crick in my neck from staring at this V-shape group of stars located in the constellation of Taurus. After I learnt to find the Hyades I was allowed to look at them through the departmental telescope which separated out the small cluster into individual stars, like looking at a crowd of people and being able to identify their faces.

Using a telescope was not just about learning to see objects in the sky, it involved a whole collection of new sensory experiences such as attempting to turn the focus dial of the eyepiece with hands so cold I could barely feel the ridges on the metal. Not breathing anywhere near the lens because the resulting condensation took minutes to clear. Not getting distracted by the reflection of my own eye regarding me, the magnified eyelashes and iris superimposed on the tiny circle of sky. Swigging from flasks of strong tea and eating peanut butter sandwiches at three o'clock in the morning to try and keep up my flagging energy. Waiting for the sky to clear when the stars were blocked from view by the inevitable clouds.

The night sky soaked into my bone-cold hands and feet, and made my neck hurt from peering through the eye piece or tilting my face upwards. Night seeped into day, made my head ache with tiredness when I returned to my bedroom and tried to get to sleep. It took up residence throughout my body, a sort of ever-present darkness that balanced out the fluorescent-lit days I spent sitting in labs and lecture halls. If those days could be stressful because of the desires and the uncertainties of being a student, the night sky provided a ballast. During this time of measuring the Hyades I started a relationship with a boy, and when I had to say goodbye to him each dusk-filled afternoon in late autumn (the time of the year when the Hyades are at their zenith and easiest to observe) he would sing 'Starry, starry night' to me.

To view the constellations night after night is to experience a kaleidoscope of associations. In the northern constellation of Andromeda there is a faint thumb-print of light, one of a very few galaxies that can be seen by the naked eye without a telescope. In Greek mythology, the gods chain Andromeda to rocks as a punishment for the hubris of her mother Cassiopeia, before she is saved from a threatening sea monster by the heroic Perseus who then marries her. The mythological Andromeda is a passive woman, seemingly without any agency over her own life and fate, and the galaxy Andromeda is hurtling towards the Milky Way, nothing can stop the two from colliding in a few billion years. This flickering to and fro between myth and science is a reminder that the sky is not a passive backdrop to our human activities, it is a theatre and a generator of thought.

As I progressed through my degree, I learned that the Sun emitted not just visible light but also radio waves which peaked and troughed in cycles I could plot on a piece of paper and explain with a mathematical equation. 'Radio star' became a graph of curved lines and data points as well as a poem.

Standing on the roof of the physics department and preparing to look at the Hyades, I would sometimes spin round and round and watch the stars rotate the opposite way. The Universe was a giant spinning top and I was at its centre. I learned that this was not true, the Universe had no centre. The boy I had fallen in love with told me he thought he might be attracted to other boys. Or not. He wasn't sure, but he would still sing to me while he tried to decide. The Universe was expanding, everything moving further away from everything else. The gaps between the galaxies would only grow larger as time flowed from the past through our present, and on into the future.

These gaps that we see between stars and galaxies are not easily explained. In principle, an infinitely large, infinitely old Universe should be as least as bright in every single direction as the surface of the Sun and wherever you look at night-time you should see light from one of the infinite number of stars. But this is not the case because the sky appears to be dark at night; individual stars are surrounded by apparently empty space. The boy left, then he came back to me. Why were we surrounded by so much darkness? Such an apparently obvious question is problematic to answer. For my degree I wrote an essay about the many possible explanations of this paradox of the dark sky. I wrote about the genius required to identify what is uncanny about the most obvious observation anyone can make of the night. Based on other people's more coherently expressed arguments, I wrote that this only appears to be a paradox because of our apparently reasonable assumptions, and in fact the Universe cannot be both infinitely large and old. Something has to give. According to the Big Bang theory, the Universe began in an explosion 13.7 billion years ago and has been expanding ever since; in this scenario there has not been enough time for the light from the most distant stars to reach us on Earth and that is one of the reasons for the darkness of the night sky. We will never be able to see all there is to see before it is carried away from us.

SUNDAY 13TH FEBRUARY

Unformed Bluebells like beansprouts around King Alfred's feet. Poisonous.

> The Itchen in spate
> through its Roman route.
> February weeds are
> tongues talking Brittonic
> under gin-clear folds.

There is a cartoon rat painted as a mural on a wall. A quiet corner of plague memories.

Runnels are made by den-building children in the thicket edge above the M3. The path at the back of the houses.

A vertiginous bridge.

Vertigo and its unsafety form an entry to a slower path in a shifted place.

That, and the first blackthorn dressed in white.

A broken post and a mud track, and suddenly downland.

A mystery object caught in thorns and barbed wire. A ball, wrangled by its hair of trailing fibres, pulling in the wind against space in a hedge tangle.

> Dented to make the
> face of an alien,
> a Grey,
> or an owl. Screaming
> an omen.

St Andrew's Chilcomb, seen across the shallow valley. A small box, uneven in age, sunk in centuries.

A red-headed boy is running. On the far-side. There is a terror in his rough run. I know his name is Michael and he is out of time. He runs to the priest at Chilcomb on an errand.

Leaving the first field, under a three-way fingerpost is a lost key in the muddy ground of the crossroads.

I begin to think the chance of rain was overstated and, in doing so, I find I have called the first, and then the heavier.

Hard breath now   pain-breath   burn breath   cold burn on the hill up from the valley floor

Sore breath   a stop for gasping   already wheezing

A Windfucker performs while I piss through a gate into its field, until the rain beats it down.

> The top is sudden
> everything is aerial.

The world becomes claggy as the wind mists the rain into horizontal lines.

I wonder if Michael sees me too.

A tumulus with a view to the white disks and geodesics of a planetarium.

> Make a circle on the land
> and the spirits will see,
> the spirits will come,
> circle   circle   a circle so
> those buried here
> can see their way back.

Beech trees now, wet with grey, silver, and black. Weeping black.

A figure twice the size of a man, made of black flame, like the black that flickers at the edge of sight when consciousness leaves. And stars within it.

On the path drowned in mud-water, floating, turning like a compass needle, two fragile white bones, still jointed,
still ligament.

This is a teaching. Standing with all my skin wet, clothes tight, drops on my eyebrows like decorations.

Circle   fill with water   float the lightest of bones   bird or mouse
for directionality   for calling the things underneath.

Crossroad Demon.

Self- replicating spheres and folds of black smoke   a column of black   the burning of a stolen car in an isolated lane   the pyre of disease in fields   the time the countryside stole the horror of the cities   impossible to fix the eye   hints   of   starlight, reaching the wet sky   tyres within tyres, no eyes.

> The cross of bridleway and lane
> these are the under ways
> overwritten by the thicker
> strokes of A-roads
> slipping beneath like ghosts.

I am a ghost on this road   or will become one.

Rain red bricks. Early morning frost. Telephone wires cross power lines under silver edges of cloud. A large dog barks in the distance. White blossom streaming over fields. I did not hear any words. For a long time there were no actual words only phrases and accents without meaning. I changed my mind. Changed my dress. Painted my fingernails under cold stars. Change is best. There are no words. Words are white blossoms streaming over fields. I am writing as fast as I can because I am not sure how long I have left. I am leaving a hurried note at the back of my drawer. Orange sunset in dormer window. A lifetime ago. An image. The disintegration of a photograph. I did not hear any words. For a long time there were no words only white noise interspersed with high frequency registers. Telephone wires cross power lines under a dark blue cloud bank. Carrion crows face the future in the oak tree on the other side of the recently ploughed field. Downpour red blocks. I talk to myself under viral skies. The words are hurried notes carried over huge distances. Time is complicit. The cuckoo in the clock. They can all hear what I am thinking. The disintegration of memory. For the time being clear night sky. For the time being kissing gate. For the time being long white dress. I like to watch because you can see others find their way around the footpaths and the horse fields and the cow fields and then you will never have to find the way yourself. It is of course better to find the way yourself and let others watch you so that they do not have to do it themselves. Towns have more rules and are therefore easier to navigate. You can follow the rain because it falls in different places depending on where you are in relation to the clouds and depending on how you are feeling. A cut crystal suspended from a window latch by nylon string. Prismatic light. Diagonal patterns. Constellations. Time elapsed and for the first time it elapsed. There are pylons in the distance. A line of old oak trees. Sparrows feeding in the recently ploughed field. Big Song is water. Big Song is white noise. Big Song is the last line of a book. I did not say anything for a very long time and I didn't hear anyone else say anything for even longer. Dirty dishes in a dirty sink. We are back there. Here. Back again. Under the dead leaves. Mouse blood on my slipper. The cat kettle the calling back. Here in the nineteen-eighties black bees feed upon the past. There are lines and colours through thick patio glass — the sound of transistor radios — a delicate balance restored. Telephone wires cross power lines under threads of fine white cloud. Car windscreen / heavy rain. The hawthorn props up the broken fence as line autocorrects. Talking about Big Song is like talking to a piece of glass.

1. ON MEETING THE MAN

Summer, twenty-five-and-a-bit years ago. The Man asked me for directions on a flooded street. I was living and working in Kolkata at the time. November, twenty-five and a bit years ago, I said goodbye to The Man. It seemed like, whatever we thought, it could not work. I was too broken, we lived in different countries and many other things. Twenty-five years ago, I married The Man.

The Mother I will mention in a little while is my late mother who, since she died in my late adolescence, has been (as in life) a peril to me. It was all broken, you see. But it didn't matter then, and it does not now.

So, I went walking. There was a man on the other side of the street, wading through water happily and going in the opposite direction and he called across to her, 'Excuse me, can you tell me the way I could get to the Blue-Sky Café?'

I was startled because he had chosen a sentence with pleasing internal rhymes (though its tetrameter was imperfect) and momentarily thought I might have imagined him. I said, 'Go straight ahead to the corner and you'll see it there.' To have attempted the beckoning symmetry of the metre really would have been a shade too far. Anyway, what I should have said was, 'Turn round and go straight ahead and you'll see it there,' because the man whirled, lost in the watery street. The ability to give inaccurate directions for the simplest of journeys was a point he raised with me later that day when we met on the same side of the street. Still, he followed me (with his own directions), to home, to the funny old house, and came to visit for a while and then never left. Later, we filled it with laughing and hollering, with crying, children, and a host of rescue creatures.

And I told The Man, 'I forgive you for the broken tetrameter.'

And he said, 'Your directions suck and why didn't you just point to the signpost?'

And I said, 'Signposts and I have a difficult history.'

Looking back, it was as if I met him in a story, stumbling across a book by a familiar author in an unfamiliar place: this was, truly, how it was, after the day in the flooded street in Kolkata. The Man had a calm eye; he didn't wake in the night, sitting bolt upright, like I did. He had faith: he had it in the palm of his hand and the heel of his shoe, and I looked at it and saw possibility and I followed him, just as he followed me. Sometimes, we fell over one another and howled as we travelled on. In another city, I watched him go out and imagined what he saw, single and indivisible: this was how it went.

Varanasi, one of the world's oldest inhabited cities. It was not his city, but I sensed he felt at home there. He sat by the river at dawn and a multitude was there, bathing and praying and offering up what they could.

Look at him. Look at how still he is.

How does he do that?

He is exceptional.

The sun hit the water and he watched the multitude quietly, not able to offer a libation, yet content to watch and bless vicariously. He bought tea and set it by my bed. Then, later, mangoes, limes, tomatoes, onions, and some olive oil from an ayurvedic medicine shop so that he could make a salad dressing of sorts. He begged a small hillock of salt; his eyes said he hoped I would be proud of what he had done. On the balcony of the room, the light was dazzling. There, he assembled breakfast for me, and called me out from my room. I sat at ease; he smoothed my hair, put on my hat, and gave me what he had made. We said little as we ate and watched the sun, still in its ascent. The colour of the Ganges changed from white and gold to the more familiar muddy brown. Now, he stood up and told me that, from now on, he would stop running, stop travelling away from and start travelling to a destination. Whenever he put one foot in front of the other, it would be with me. I understood and that was that. There were smiles of complicity.

But still, I told you I was broken.

'Stay with me.'

'I don't know if I can. I am broken. I was never made properly. There is more than one of me.'

'And you think any of that bothers me?'

In the lanes below, the monkeys chattered. They could smell the food he had prepared and were ready to steal. He spoke a prayer. Then he said: 'And again and again, I don't care who you are and if you are more than one,' he said. Then: 'Broken is beautiful, too. Don't you know that?'

'What about my dead mother? She's still here, all the time, chattering in my ear, telling me how worthless I am, what a little canker I am.'

'We'll ignore her.'

'And The Other?'

'He's fine. He prefers other people to you, so you have an out there.'

'I hurt myself.'

'I'll stanch the blood or maybe just tie you up to stop you doing it.'

'That sounds alluring,' said I. Then, 'What about God who is – Dead if He ever Existed?'

And The Man said, 'He is alive. He was down by the river.'

May I offer a digression?

When he was ten, The Man happened to be in an elevator in a hotel in Dallas, Texas. In walked a tall man; the boy looked at the man's shoes. From there, it was a long way up, but look he did. The boy saw that it was Johnny Cash. No, he must be wrong. But hang on, Johnny Cash must have had to ride in an elevator some time, so the boy looked again. He nudged his little brother, 'Curtis, I think it's Johnny Cash.' Maybe the man heard him, maybe not. But he bent low and smiled a warm, wide smile and said, 'Helllllllo boys.'

The child was star-struck and cannot remember if he said hello back. Little brother was possibly unmoved, being too young and green to comprehend that Johnny Cash was not to be seen riding in an elevator with you any day of the week. Cash was, like him, a Southern man. Little links kind of went in deep: faith and difficulty and broken things and joy. And riding in that elevator. I noticed that The Man would listen and feel at home; saw that Cash was flawed, powerful and weak. He had struggled with addiction and the darkest of insecurities. Cash had faith that was angry and brave and music that haunted even when it jangled. In a quiet moment, he picked 'Down There by the Train' with its invocation to meet him if you had travelled the low road; if, broken and sinning, you had passed the same way.

There are times when the puzzles and the headaches just drift away: I met The Man and he had a faith that was flawed and wanting and made sense, now that was like moisture on my parched and callow soul and for a while it washed away my feeling of the absurdity and booted those who created it out of the door. It was temporary, but it was beautiful while it lasted. It was utterly beautiful, and I had the tiniest of notions that one day it would come back. One fine day when golden light breaks through the mist and, as in the song, Judas Iscariot, betrayer of Jesus, carries John Wilkes Booth, assassin of Abraham Lincoln; when rifts are healed and the person who hated you forgives you.

Teardrops fell like summer tempests and I, glimpsing the world through another's eyes, (sometime while listening to Johnny Cash) sensed possibility and found it both gorgeous and painful.

Oh, when The Man followed me first, there was much wailing and gnashing of teeth from both families once everyone began to understand that he might be staying. For issuing from tomorrow, come today and other people, when time is no longer away.

The Mother was there, though dead, inviting them all out, smilingly, winningly, 'Come and see my bitch daughter. Look what she's done now.' I felt it acutely, and it is very difficult to explain this sort of thing to others, as if my life were magical realism, the dead and the living intertwined.

A SPRIG OF A FRUITED OLIVE
— travels with 'Olives' by A. E. Stallings and the Portuguese
Nobel Laureate José Saramago

OLIVES have always been markers for memorable times during my life. As episodic palate cleansers in Venice, in dimly lit bars in Manhattan, or in the shady hills of Valldemossa in Mallorca; whether swilled in the mouth or smashed into cool aromatic vermouth with vodka, they are almost anaesthetic when steeped in 80 proof, but even devoured as solo morsels, they can numb a multitude of painful little life-cuts.

In her poem 'Olives', poet A. E. Stallings contrasts her perception of the fruits of the venerable olive tree with the minutiae of her daily existence. The poem appears in a collection of the same name, set against a backdrop of ancient myth. So it goes, 'Sometimes a craving comes for salt, not sweet / For fruits that you can eat / Only if pickled in a vat of tears', which reminds me how much I identified with those words back when my carefully constructed life began to disintegrate.

At various times, olives have accompanied the easy veil of early-stage tipsiness like small green bridesmaids. They are plain yet also decadent. Their polyphenols bind to secrets I have never told anyone sober. At the taste of a dirty martini, I conjure my reckless and impulsive twenties; in Turin, Barcelona, the Vieux-Port de Marseille, or Vancouver. The late nights and sunrises. Those bitter moments of sudden clarity.

I see rickety pavement café tables pushed close together, the gritty dust of a strange city underfoot, and I wonder when it was I savoured it first? An olive dropped like a lush penny into a frozen well, liquid smoking as swirls of brine and flecks of ice intermingle. What was its allure, this deep and dark-hearted pitted gem, so brash, and so unyielding? At the same time, I question what caused me to choose this frequently exhilarating, often discomforting path of travel and solitude I followed for so long.

§

I travel to Mallorca at twenty-nine with my mother and we stay in the Hotel Continental outside Valldemossa. It is a cliff-side hotel with sliding balcony doors that open to an uninterrupted view of an aching blue Mediterranean Sea. I am a woman that I hardly recognise now. With a recent blunt fringe and wearing pink wayfarers which do not suit me, I am in disguise in my own life — listless, flighty, seeking respite from a marriage that I have yet to exit and sick to my briny extremities with ill-advised desire for a person who will never love me in the way I require.

It is the first time I confide in my mother that my careful façade of happiness is just that, although, as mothers do, she has had her suspicions. I write out Spanish verbs in a spiral notebook on my sun-lounger by the salt-water swimming pool carved into bleached stone. I still harbour a belief I will move to this green-spun Balearic island and put down roots amongst the Arbequina in the rich soils of the Soller valley, but this dream was becoming more and more distant, as though I have no business expecting things to turn out well. My mother reminds me in her judicious way that I can hope for more.

The virtue of the great olive tree is extolled throughout the Tramuntana basin and I respect its longevity, its unabashed plainness, its gnarled and knotty character. In contrast, I find myself sincerely lacking. I am yet to be tested.

§

In Stallings' olives of 'Brown greens and purple browns, the blacks and blues / That chart the slow chromatics of a bruise,' I recall the emotional bruises I bear. Bruises borne of the frustration of marital disconnection and complicated by an ill-judged friendship with an Italian man-child I had become entangled with in Genoa, someone I believed saw me in a way my ex-husband did not. I didn't seek a transition into a new relationship, or to be fully understood by anybody, but the slow chromatics of a bruise is an apt way to describe the agonising realisation as it dawns that you are in danger of uprooting your entire existence on a whim. Sometimes it doesn't even feel dangerous or particularly terrifying; it just feels necessary. Like something you have to do in order to keep breathing.

In Deia, there lives a venerable member of the native Empeltre Mallorquina species that was once described as 'best monumental olive tree' in Spain and awarded a prize for maturity and resistance having lived to over 1,100 years old. One day I go there to observe it in its habitat. Thick trunked, hard-working, ashen, earthen-brown and leafy, and bearing a fruit that is as different to its succulent and rainbow-hued cousins — the apples, grapes and pears — as it can get. I stand next to it to admire its ancient ego, olives imbued with a solid practicality that I envy. They possess a certain perspicacity, being at once nothing special and yet somehow exotic, I have sought to emulate myself. I enjoyed the anonymity of starting again in strange places and the thrill of bypassing language barriers and figuring out the false cognates. In Nice, in the Côte d'Azur or San Remo on the Ligurian coast, my regular-girl Kentish-ness translated to something unique and potentially intriguing in a way it didn't at home.

The fruits of these trees are abundant and foreign, unadorned and simple with typical flavours of salt, pine, and nut butter that are anything but ordinary when combined with insight and experience. Way back before I met my ex-husband — as well as throughout our marriage, and the years after we separated — I harboured a deep desire to move to Mallorca. I recognised that the likelihood of living that life was becoming more and more distant. As for the olives — the Arbequina, the Picual, and Mallorquina, their complexity grows as you consider them. Though astringent and sharp when under-ripe and raw, if too mature they collapse to flavourless mush. There is an adventure to be found in discovering the perfect time; when an object speaks of its character with wit and verve, but also does not slide into mawkish nostalgia.

During that trip with my mother, I start to understand what I have been sacrificing to be with somebody who did not support my ambition to write and to whom, because of the logistics of our careers, I was becoming more of a stranger.

If there is a phrase that sums up this period of my life, it is 'Paradigmatic summers that decline / Like singular archaic nouns, the troops / Of hours in retreat.' I had existed for years bouncing from summer to summer, from rich yacht enclaves of the Mediterranean to even richer islands like St Barths and Virgin Gorda in the Caribbean, never stopping to examine the trajectory my life was taking. I question, on that trip, when I will find the perfect age in which to stand comfortably in my skin without binding myself to a relationship which cannot serve me. As I approach thirty, what will it cost me to begin all over again?

INTRODUCTION

The physical world is God's body.

— Spinoza

On the road to Damascus, Paul the Apostle saw a blinding light. A ray of magneto-acoustic plasma spoke with the voice of God. The splintering that entered the mind of Paul the Apostle was blissful and viridian. The entire universe permeates with an endless light. As researchers, we have received the same transmission. We understand these transmissions as an ongoing communication with an entity known only as OBIDOS, or *the walled city*. The channel of communication with OBIDOS was established through our discovery of PSY-V-E. The synthesis of these three drugs acts as an inter-dimensional chiasma. An optic nerve was flung out into the outer constellations and we passed through its dreaming thread, along the twenty-eight zodiac mansions.

OBIDOS operates like an eyeball: a visual pathway that moves beyond our consciousness and reaches the faintest of stars, our pale dead fathers. Our pituitary glands sprouted like cyclopic stalks which saw the mitochondrial disease of living. But now we are so clean. Bathed in fonts of sapphire water upon the Kangchenjunga Mountain, we have entered the mind of OBIDOS through a gateway of impossible glass, swam through and inside the walled fortress. Its walls are silent and green-blue. We sleep in piles of warm black snakes. An evening call to prayer rouses us from our slumber. The darkness is so bright here.

Myself and Participant Y follow dreamers now. We see Ptolemy levitating from his bed in the second century, guided by Urania, daughter of Mnemosyne. He sleepwalks from his Alexandrian home, down into the city. Night falls upon our skin as we wander through ashen chasms in the mountainside. A Babylonian moon climbs into the sky surrounded by the pink flowers of embarrassed cacti. A minotaur faints inside clouds of violets. We undress before his purple lullabies, the kindness of flowers. We gorge on red clay at our feet.

The toxic Manchester pollution has solidified into archways, septic oils of rainbows. There are tendrils in the wall of the apartment. Twitching ball of spider nerves. Happily, we nail ganglia to the floor. OBIDOS confirmed to us the monism of Spinoza, a thought that guided modern physics through its century-long anxiety attack. There is only one continuum and we live inside its quantum corpse. We wander through its digestive system, lungs and urine. OBIDOS is the trembling retina. Sat with Participant Y, we hear the distant mumble of traffic beneath the window. We witness the necrotic shiver of a table lamp. A crease in a cushion is still the Dead Sea.

There are two researchers for this study but I will submit only my own account. During each experiment, Participant Y had an almost identical experience. He has produced a number of visual works that seem to confirm empirically that we have encountered an entity beyond our pathetic grasp of time and space. A glowing Gemini. We are reborn like twins beneath the alien ray. Our minds have entwined with Xolotl; the invisible brother of Quetzalcoatl. There is a walled city with two suns above a beautiful courtyard. The smell of jasmine dances in the air. We live in so many worlds now, thanks to the visitor. One day, a stranger entered our apartment. We sat patiently and listened to his story. We only ask for the same. Our claims might be outrageous but we can only be humble messengers. It is the responsibility of others to accept or deny. When Lot's wife turned back to look at Sodom, she saw the entire city being eaten by a pink-red dragon descended from an obsidian sun. The angels petrified her body into salt because seeing is always transgression. We have chosen to look at the shameless city. In the sky above Tenochtitlan, there dances an Aztec palace filled with blood and buzzards, a shining plateau of bird viscera. Quetzalcoatl asked the villagers for the killed souls of butterflies and hummingbirds. The dawn beyond them was viridian glow. Come closer, my friend. Drink from the invisible hand of OBIDOS. Slowly, upon the video screen, the eye begins to opens.

INSTRUCTIONS

1.   Participant X and Y took $\approx$ 0.5mg of PSY-V-E drug in liquid form.

2.   A glass of water was placed in front of each participant.

3.   Both participants sat on a chair facing their glass.

4.   A stopwatch and video recording on iPhone of Participant X started.

5.   A 10kg barbell weight was rested on the lap on each participant.

INTRODUCTION

Awards! They always give out awards! I can't believe it. Greatest Fascist Dictator: Adolf Hitler...
— Alvy Singer, *Annie Hall*

In my first week at Nottingham University in 1975, the writer Stanley Middleton came to talk about his novel *Holiday*. Eager to meet a 'real writer' for the first time, I arrived at the event early – but found myself completely unable to go through the door, somehow feeling that I did not have the right to enter. British society is very good at persuading people to think that we are not allowed in, that culture belongs to others who are better qualified by class and money and culture and geography and education.

Much of my working life over the last forty years has been spent trying to hold the doors open as widely as possible for others who want to step inside – in university adult education, in schools, prisons and community projects. I have worked in over 400 schools and a dozen prisons; for ten years I edited a weekly column of readers' poems in the Middlesbrough *Evening Gazette*; I ran the Writearound Community Writing Festival in Cleveland (1989-2000), the T-junction International Poetry Festival in Middlesbrough (2014-18) and the Ripon Poetry Festival (2017-24); I wrote a monthly poetry column in the *Morning Star* from 2004-22, and for many years edited the 'poem of the week' feature in the paper. I helped run Teesside community-publishers Mudfog Books from 1993 to 2003, since when I have edited Smokestack Books. For the last six years I have been one of the judges of the Culture Matters annual Bread and Roses poetry competition sponsored by UNITE. The essays and reviews in this book can only be understood in this context.

I have chosen to reprint these pieces out of the several hundred book-reviews I have written since 1980, because they express a kind of developing argument with the world of British poetry – specifically regarding issues of access, privilege and ownership.

During that time large sections of British economic life have been moved out of common ownership into private hands, rationed by price or simply closed down. The democratic process is blocked by inequality, authoritarianism, deceit and a narrow ideological consensus. British cultural life is blocked by the values of big business and show business.

The result is an atomised, unwelcoming and unfriendly poetry scene whose inaccessibility is hardly disguised by ritual declarations about diversity and inclusion. Conversations about poetry have been replaced by conversations about poets, discussions of tradition by accusations of plagiarism, and the language of literary criticism by the language of press-releases promoting corporate prizes and celebrity book-festivals. As Mark Fisher once put it, 'all that is solid melts into PR':

> Over the past thirty years capitalist realism has successfully installed a "business ontology" in which it is simply obvious that everything in society... should be run as a business... conditioning not only the production of culture but also the regulation of work and education, and acting as a kind of invisible barrier constraining thought and action.

Jonathan Davidson has called this the 'poetry-industrial complex', a tightly controlled market in which high-profile prizes 'help select the most profitable lines of investment' for corporate publishers:

> Competitions generate the cannon fodder of the perennially disappointed, while providing the industry with its national heroes. Slim volumes are barely read but are a useful means of stoking the fires of ambition for the unpublished and are also a means of creating value through scarcity, a scarcity that is further inflated through a prize culture.

The US poet Amanda Gorman was recently invited to chair the New York Met Gala (together with singer Billie Eilish, actor Timothée Chalamet and tennis-player Naomi Osaka). Photographed by Annie Leibovitz for the cover of *Vogue*, Amanda Gorman is now an Estée Lauder 'global changemaker'. Meanwhile, the National Poetry Library in London recently hosted an exhibition 'Poets in Vogue', of clothes worn by famous twentieth-century poets – a skirt worn by Sylvia Plath on a visit to Paris, a kaftan like one worn by Audre Lorde after her mastectomy, a red dress like one sometimes worn by Anne Sexton at poetry readings. This feels like a door that is still firmly locked.

Today there are only three kinds of poet: 'Prize-winning Poet', 'Emerging Poet' (hasn't yet won a prize) and 'Rising Poet' (hasn't yet published a book). A few years ago, when I gave a series of readings in the US, I was embarrassed to find that I was introduced everywhere as an 'award-winning English poet'. What other kind could there be? Juliana Spahr and Stephanie Young have described the North American system of poetry prizes thus:

> Some days we think of poetry as a dead antelope and poets as wolves, hyenas, and cayotes who come to fight over the innards, teeth bared, growling. Some days we think of poetry as the centre panel of Bosch's *Garden of Earthly* delights with poets as the naked libertines in small groups that notice only each other, some immersed in a pool balancing apples on their heads, some floating together in a bubble, others riding on the backs of birds.

The essays in this book were written in the belief that poetry is essentially a public and collective expression of emotionally shared symbolic meanings. The word 'symbol' is derived from the Greek word *symbolon*; in ancient Greece, two friends sharing hospitality would break a piece of pottery in half, each keeping one piece as a token of friendship and recognition. The critic Byung-Chul Han has argued that the writing and reading of poetry is itself a kind of ritual of social exchange:

> According to the myth related by Aristophanes in Plato's *Symposium*, humans were originally globular beings with two faces and four

legs. Because they were so unruly, Zeus sought to weaken them by dividing them in two. Ever since their division, humans have been *symbola*, longing for their other half, longing for a healing wholeness.

A poem is an exchange of factual and emotional and imaginative information. It is also a potential exchange of trust, vulnerability and kindness. The writer of a poem has to trust that strangers will treat kindly their best attempt to express, describe, imagine and understand the world. The reader has to trust that the writer will treat them kindly by helping them to make sense of and enjoy a poem that they have never seen before. Each relies on the other's understanding that this exchange is both difficult and important. Writers and readers have to listen to each other carefully. But it is increasingly hard to hear anything against the constant white noise of PR and hyperbolic praise competing for ownership over the Next Big Thing.

The poet Randall Swingler once put it like this:

> It must always be remembered that poetry is older and simpler than any other form of language. It fulfils, in fact, the original function of language, intended by its rhythmical character to keep people together, to organise their powers into a unity, to make them aware of their common nature and interest, their essential community one with another... as imagination is the primary function of the mind so poetry maintains the primary function of language, of stimulating social activity in persons engaged together in a common task. Hence the reaping-songs, and the sea-shanties, the ballads and the early epics, which are all of war, religious rites or navigation, the only activities which the group still pursued as a unity. The simplicity of poetry is the concrete force of its symbols: and so, much of modern verse-writing, since it does not subserve this primary function, cannot be classed as poetry at all... a different art, if you like, but not poetry. The art perhaps of correspondence or the art of games, which may be witty, pathetic, ingenious, sentimental, within the limits of those arts. Whatever poetry is, it is not a magpies' nest... What has happened to poetry then? Simply that in a profit-making society there is no place for it, where all social functions are increasingly divided into individual specialization, and the function of poetry is gradually eliminated.

Poetry is a way of knowing ourselves and others better, of sharing and extending the common ownership of experience, feeling and language, of resisting the forces that would divide us. Poetry is a social production or it is nothing at all. It is not a competition. It is not a career. It is not private property. Poetry belongs to everyone, not just to those with an agent, a back-story, a Creative Writing MA, a shiny prize and an Instagram following. The doors still need kicking down.

— North Yorkshire 2024

7 years later, we're still laying out our unrest